TEXTBOOK OF PLANT CHEMISTRY

TEXTBOOK OF PLANT CHEMISTRY

By
Dr. Pooja
Dept. of Botany
R.C.C. College
Ghaziabad (U.P.)
(India)

DISCOVERY PUBLISHING HOUSE PVT. LTD.
NEW DELHI-110 002

Published by:
Namit Wasan

DISCOVERY PUBLISHING HOUSE PVT. LTD.
4383/4B, Ansari Road, Darya Ganj
New Delhi-110 002 (India)
Phone : +91-11-23279245; 23253475; 43596065
E-mail : discoverybooksindia@gmail.com
discoverypublishinghouse@gmail.com
namitwasan9@gmail.com
web : www.discoverypublishinggroup.com

***Reprinted:* 2020**

***First Edition:* 2011**

ISBN: 978-81-8356-848-7

Textbook of Plant Chemistry

Printed at:
Infinity Imaging Systems
Delhi

Preface

Plants are a major group of living things (about 300,000 species), including familiar organisms such as trees, flowers, herbs, and ferns. Aristotle divided all living things between plants, which generally do not move or have sensory organs, and animals. In Linnaeus' system, these became the Kingdoms Vegetabilia (later Plantae) and Animalia. Since then, it has become clear that the Plantae as originally defined included several unrelated groups, and the fungi and several groups of algae were removed to new kingdoms. However, these are still often considered plants in many contexts. Indeed, any attempt to match "plant" with a single taxon is doomed to fail, because plant is a vaguely defined concept unrelated to the presumed phylogenic concepts on which modern taxonomy is based.

Vascular plants first appeared during the Silurian period, and by the Devonian had diversified and spread into many different land environments. They have a number of adaptations that allowed them to overcome the limitations of the bryophytes. These include a cuticle resistant to desiccation, and vascular tissues which transport water throughout the organism. In many the sporophyte acts as a separate individual, while the gametophyte remains small.

The first primitive seed plants, Pteridosperms (seed ferns) and Cordaites, both groups now extinct, appeared in the late Devonian and diversified through the Carboniferous, with further evolution through the Permian and Triassic periods. In these the gametophyte stage is completely reduced, and the sporophyte begins life inside an enclosure called a seed, which develops while on the parent plant, and with fertilization by means of pollen grains. Whereas other vascular plants, such as ferns, reproduce by means of spores and so need moisture to develop, some seed plants can survive and reproduce in extremely arid conditions.

Author

Contents

Preface

1. Introduction 1

Embryophytes; Algae and Fungi; Importance; Growth; Fossils; Current Definitions of "Plant"; Algae; Fungi; Diversity; Life Processes; Factors Affecting Growth; Internal Distribution; Ecology; Distribution; Ecological Relationships; Importance; Food; Non-food Products; Aesthetic Uses; Scientific and Cultural Uses; Negative Effects

2. Plant Physiology 17

Scope; Biochemistry of Plants; Constituent Elements; Pigments; Signals and Regulators; Environmental Physiology; History; Economic Applications

3. Plant Morphology 30

Scope; A Comparative Science; Vegetative and Reproductive Characters; Plant Anatomy; Structural Divisions; History

4. Wood Anatomy 43

Bark; Botanic Description; Periderm; Rhytidome; Uses; Bark Chip Extraction; Bark Removal; Bark Repair; Phloem; Structure; Function; Origin; Wood; Different Woods; Colour; Water Content

5. Root 67

Root Growth; Types of Roots; Specialized Roots; Rooting Depths; Root Architecture; Evolutionary History; Economic Importance; Plant Cutting; Technique; Types of Cuttings; Providing the Right Soil; Providing the Right Humidity; Rooting Substance; Homemade Rooting Supplements; Using Rooting Hormone or Supplement; Stem Cuttings; Grafting; Techniques; Renewing Fusion; Natural Grafting; Scientific Uses; Herbaceous Grafting

6. Plant Hormone 86

Characteristics; Classes of Plant Hormones; Potential Medical Applications; Hormones and Plant Propagation

7. Cell Membranes 97

The Plasma Membrane; Integral Membrane Proteins; Peripheral Membrane Proteins; The Nucleus; The Nuclear Envelope; Chromatin; Nucleosomes; Histone Modifications; Histone Variants; Chromosome Territories; "Kissing" Chromosomes; Euchromatin versus Heterochromatin; Heterochromatin; Euchro-matin; Nucleosomes and Transcription; The Nucleolus; Nuclear Pore Complexes (NPCs); Import into the Nucleus; Export from the Nucleus; Nucleoplasm; Cellular Respiration; Mitochondria; The Citric Acid Cycle; The Electron

Transport Chain; Chemiosmosis in Mitochondria; How many ATPs?; Mitochondrial DNA (mtDNA); The Cytoskeleton; Actin Filaments; Intermediate Filaments; Microtubules; Microtubule Motors; Centrosome; Centrioles; Cilia and Flagella; Primary Cilia

8. Chlorophyll **125**

Chlorophyll and Photosynthesis; Chemical Structure; Spectrophotometry; Biosynthesis; Culinary Use; Pigments

9. Photosynthesis **131**

Leaves and Leaf Structure; The Nature of Light; Chlorophyll and Accessory Pigments; The Structure of the Chloroplast and Photo synthetic Membranes; Stages of Photosynthesis; C-4 Pathway; The Carbon Cycle

10. Porphyrin **141**

Complexes of Porphyrins and Related Molecules; Laboratory Synthesis; Biosynthesis; Applications; Porphyria; Signs and Symptoms; Diagnosis

11. Plant Defense Against Herbivory **149**

Plant Evolution; Types; Costs and Benefits; Importance to Humans; Pharmaceutical

12. Plant Medicines **166**

Introduction; Herbal use 60,000 Years Ago; Patent Laws Drive Medicinal Development; Drugs are often Dangerous; Plant Medicines, Safer and Time-tested; Plants and Humans Share Similarities; Synthetic Drugs are Foreign to the Body; Plants can be Dangerous too; What Are Herbs?; Drugs of Plant Origin; The other Side of Plant Medicines;

13. Major Groups of Chemicals for Plant Disease Control **175**

Inorganic Fungicides; Organic Fungicides; Antibiotics; Systemic Fungicides; Fumigants

14. Photoperiodism **180**

Photoperiodism in a Short-day Plant; Phytochrome; The Hourglass Model; Problems with the Hourglass Model; The Circadian Rhythm Model; Long-Day Plants; Constans messenger RNA (mRNA); Short-Day Plants; Trees; Animal Responses; Seasonal Responses; Mechanisms

15. Photomorphogenesis **191**

UV Systems; Analysis of Photomorphogenesis; Phytochrome; Cryptochrome; HY5; COP1 and the COP9 Signalsome; Hormones; Phototropin

16. Circadian Rhythm **200**

History; Criteria; Origin; Importance in Animals; Biological Clock in Mammals; Outside the "Master Clock"; Light and the Biological Clock; The Myth of the 25-hour Day; The Human Circadian Period; Disruption

Index ***211***

Introduction

Plants are a major group of living things (about 300,000 species), including familiar organisms such as trees, flowers, herbs, and ferns. Aristotle divided all living things between plants, which generally do not move or have sensory organs, and animals. In Linnaeus' system, these became the Kingdoms Vegetabilia (later Plantae) and Animalia. Since then, it has become clear that the Plantae as originally defined included several unrelated groups, and the fungi and several groups of algae were removed to new kingdoms. However, these are still often considered plants in many contexts. Indeed, any attempt to match "plant" with a single taxon is doomed to fail, because plant is a vaguely defined concept unrelated to the presumed phylogenic concepts on which modern taxonomy is based.

Embryophytes

Most familiar are the multicellular land plants, called embryophytes. They include the vascular plants, plants with full systems of leaves, stems, and roots. They also include a few of their close relatives, often called *bryophytes*, of which mosses are the most common.

All of these plants have eukaryotic cells with cell walls composed of cellulose, and most obtain their energy through photosynthesis, using light and carbon dioxide to synthesize food. About 300 plant species do not photosynthesize but are parasites on other species of photosynthetic plants. Plants are distinguished from green algae, from which they evolved, by having specialized reproductive organs protected by non-reproductive tissues.

Bryophytes first appeared during the early Palaeozoic. They can only survive in moist environments, and remain small throughout their life-cycle. This involves an alternation between two generations: a haploid stage, called the gametophyte, and a diploid stage, called the sporophyte. The sporophyte is short-lived and remains dependent on its parent.

Vascular plants first appeared during the Silurian period, and by the Devonian had diversified and spread into many different land environments. They have a number of adaptations that allowed them to overcome the limitations of the bryophytes. These include a cuticle resistant to desiccation, and vascular tissues which transport water throughout the organism. In many the sporophyte acts as a separate individual, while the gametophyte remains small.

The first primitive seed plants, Pteridosperms (seed ferns) and Cordaites, both groups now extinct, appeared in the late Devonian and diversified through the Carboniferous, with further evolution through the Permian and Triassic periods. In these the gametophyte stage is completely reduced, and the sporophyte begins life inside an enclosure called a seed, which develops while on the parent plant, and with fertilisation by means of pollen grains. Whereas other vascular plants, such as ferns, reproduce by means of spores and so need moisture to develop, some seed plants can survive and reproduce in extremely arid conditions.

Early seed plants are referred to as gymnosperms (naked seeds), as the seed embryo is not enclosed in a protective structure at pollination, with the pollen landing directly on the embryo. Four surviving groups remain widespread now, particularly the conifers, which are dominant trees in several biomes. The angiosperms, comprising the flowering plants, were the last major group of plants to appear, emerging from within the gymnosperms during the Jurassic and diversifying rapidly during the Cretaceous. These differ in that the seed embryo is enclosed, so the pollen has to grow a tube to penetrate the protective seed coat; they are the predominant group of flora in most biomes today.

Algae and Fungi

The algae comprise several different groups of organisms that produce energy through photosynthesis. The most conspicuous are the seaweeds, multicellular algae that often closely resemble terrestrial plants, found among the green, red, and brown algae. These and other algal groups also include various single-called creatures and forms that are simple collections of cells, without differentiated tissues. Many can move about, and some have even lost their ability to photosynthesize; when first discovered, these were considered as both plants and animals.

The embryophytes developed from green algae; the two are collectively referred to as the green plants or Viridaeplantae. The kingdom Plantae is now usually taken to mean this monophyletic group, as shown above. With a few exceptions among the green algae, all such forms have cell walls containing cellulose and chloroplasts containing chlorophylls *a* and *b*, and store food in the form of starch. They undergo closed mitosis without centrioles, and typically have mitochondria with flat cristae.

The chloroplasts of green plants are surrounded by two membranes, suggesting they originated directly from endosymbiotic cyanobacteria. The same is true of the red algae, and the two groups are generally believed to have a common origin. In contrast, most other algae have chloroplasts with three or four membranes. They are not in general close relatives of the green plants, acquiring chloroplasts separately from ingested or symbiotic green and red algae.

Unlike embryophytes and algae, fungi are not photosynthetic, but are saprophytes: they obtain their food by breaking down and absorbing surrounding materials. Most fungi are formed by microscopic tubes called hyphae, which may or may not be divided into cells but contain eukaryotic nuclei. Fruiting bodies, of which mushrooms are the most familiar, are actually only the reproductive structures of fungi. They are not related to any of the photosynthetic groups, but are close relatives of animals.

Importance

The photosynthesis and carbon fixation conducted by land plants and algae are the ultimate source of energy and organic material in nearly all habitats. These processes also radically changed the composition of the Earth's atmosphere, which as a result contains a large proportion of oxygen. Animals and most other organisms are aerobic, relying on oxygen; those that do not are confined to relatively few, anaerobic environments.

Much of human nutrition depends on cereals. Other plants that are eaten include fruits, vegetables, herbs, and spices. Some vascular plants, referred to as trees and shrubs, produce woody stems and are an important source of building material. A number of plants are used decoratively, including a variety of flowers.

Growth

Simple plants like algae may have short life spans as individuals, but their populations are commonly seasonal.

Other plants may be organized according to their seasonal growth pattern:

- **Annual:** live and reproduce within one growing season.
- **Biennial:** live for two growing seasons; usually reproduce in second year.
- **Perennial:** live for many growing seasons; continue to reproduce once mature.

Among the vascular plants, perennials include both evergreens that keep their leaves the entire year, and deciduous plants which lose their leaves for some part. In temperate and boreal climates, they generally lose their leaves during the winter; many tropical plants lose their leaves during the dry season.

The growth rate of plants is extremely variable. Some mosses grow less than 1 μm/h, while most trees grow 25-250 μm/h. Some climbing species, such as kudzu, which do not need to produce thick supportive tissue, may grow up to 12500 μm/h.

Fossils

Plant fossils include roots, wood, leaves, seeds, fruit, pollen, spores and amber (the fossilized resin produced by some plants). Fossil land plants are recorded in terrestrial, lacustrine, fluvial and nearshore marine sediments. Pollen, spores and algae (dinoflagellates and acritarchs) are used for dating sedimentary rock sequences. The remains of fossil plants are not as common as fossil animals, although plant fossils are locally abundant in many regions worldwide.

Early fossil plants are well known from the Devonian period, including the chert of Rhynie in Aberdeenshire, Scotland. The best preserved examples, from which their cellular construction has been described, have been found at this locality. The preservation is so perfect that sections of these ancient plants show the individual cells within the plant tissue. The Devonian period also saw the evolution of what many believe to be the first modern tree, *Archaeopteris*. This fern-like tree combined a woody trunk with the fronds of a fern, but produced no seeds.

The Coal Measures are a major source of Palaeozoic plant fossils, with many groups of plants in existence at this time. The spoil heaps of coal mines are the best places to collect; coal itself is the remains of fossilised plants, though structural detail of the plant fossils is rarely visible in coal. In the Fossil Forest at Victoria Park in Glasgow, Scotland, the stumps of *Lepidodendron* trees are found in their original growth positions.

The fossilized remains of conifer and angiosperm roots, stems and branches may be locally abundant in lake and inshore sedimentary rocks from the Mesozoic and Caenozoic eras. Sequoia and its allies, magnolia, oak, and palms are often found.

Petrified wood is common in some parts of the world, and is most frequently found in arid or desert areas were it is more readily exposed by erosion. Petrified wood is often heavily silicified (the organic material replaced by silicon dioxide), and the impregnated tissue is often preserved in fine detail. Such specimens may be cut and polished using lapidary equipment. Fossil forests of petrified wood have been found in all continents.

Fossils of seed ferns such as *Glossopteris* are widely distributed throughout several continents of the southern hemisphere, a fact that gave support to Alfred Wegener's early ideas regarding Continental drift theory.

Plants are living organisms belonging to the kingdom Plantae. They include familiar organisms such as trees, herbs, bushes, grasses, vines, ferns, mosses, and green algae. About 350,000 species of plants, defined as seed plants, bryophytes, ferns and fern allies, are estimated to exist currently. As of 2004, some 287,655 species had been identified, of which 258,650 are flowering and 18,000 bryophytes . Green plants, sometimes called metaphytes or *viridiplantae*, obtain most of their energy from sunlight via a process called photosynthesis.

Current Definitions of "Plant"

When the name Plantae or plants is applied to a specific taxon, it is usually referring to one of three concepts. From smallest to largest in inclusiveness.

- *Land plants*, also known as Embryophyta or Metaphyta. As the narrowest of plant categories, this is further delineated below.
- *Green plants* - also known as Viridiplantae, Viridiphyta or Chlorobionta - comprise the above Embryophytes, Charophyta (i.e., primitive stoneworts), and Chlorophyta (i.e., green algae such as sea lettuce). It is this clade which is mainly the subject of this article.
- *Archaeplastida* - also known as Plantae *sensu lato*, Plastida or Primoplantae - comprises the green plants above, as well as Rhodophyta (red algae) and Glaucophyta (simple glaucophyte algae). As the broadest plant clade, this comprises most of the eukaryotes that eons ago acquired their chloroplasts directly by engulfing cyanobacteria.

Outside of formal scientific contexts, the term "plant" implies an association with certain traits, such as multicellularity, cellulose, and photosynthesis. Many of the classification controversies involve organisms that are rarely encountered and are of minimal apparent economic significance, but are crucial in developing an understanding of the evolution of modern flora.

Algae

Most algae are no longer classified within the Kingdom Plantae. The algae comprise several different groups of organisms that produce energy through photosynthesis, each of which arose independently from separate non-photosynthetic ancestors. Most conspicuous among the algae are the seaweeds, multicellular algae that may roughly resemble terrestrial plants, but are classified among the green, red, and brown algae. Each of these algal groups also includes various microscopic and single-celled organisms.

The two groups of green algae are the closest relatives of land plants (embryophytes). The first of these groups is the Charophyta (desmids and stoneworts), from which the embryophytes developed. The sister group to the combined embryophytes and charophytes is the other group of green algae, Chlorophyta, and this more inclusive group is collectively referred to as the green plants or Viridiplantae. The Kingdom Plantae is often taken to mean this monophyletic grouping. With a few exceptions among the green algae, all such forms have cell walls containing cellulose, have chloroplasts containing chlorophylls *a* and *b*, and store food in the form of starch. They undergo closed mitosis without centrioles, and typically have mitochondria with flat cristae.

The chloroplasts of green plants are surrounded by two membranes, suggesting they originated directly from endosymbiotic cyanobacteria. The same is true of two additional groups of algae: the Rhodophyta (red algae) and Glaucophyta. All three groups together are generally believed to have a common origin, and so are classified together in the taxon Archaeplastida. In contrast, most other algae (e.g. heterokonts, haptophytes, dinoflagellates, and euglenids) have chloroplasts with three or four surrounding membranes. They are not close relatives of the green plants, presumably acquiring chloroplasts separately from ingested or symbiotic green and red algae.

Fungi

Fungi were previously included in the plant kingdom, but are now seen to be more closely related to animals.

Unlike embryophytes and algae which are generally photosynthetic, fungi are often saprotrophs: obtaining food by breaking down and absorbing surrounding materials. Most fungi are formed by microscopic structures called hyphae, which may or may not be divided into cells but contain eukaryotic nuclei. Fruiting bodies, of which mushrooms are most familiar, are the reproductive structures of fungi. They are not related to any of the photosynthetic groups, but are close relatives of animals. Therefore, the fungi are in a kingdom of their own.

Diversity

About 350,000 species of plants, defined as seed plants, bryophytes, ferns and fern allies, are estimated to exist currently. As of 2004, some 287,655 species had been identified, of which 258,650 are flowering plants, 16,000 bryophytes, 11,000 ferns and 8,000 green algae.

LIFE PROCESSES

Growth

Most of the solid material in a plant is taken from the atmosphere. Through a process known as photosynthesis, plants use the energy in sunlight to convert carbon dioxide from the atmosphere, plus water, into simple sugars. These sugars are then used as building blocks and form the main structural component of the plant. Chlorophyll, a green-colored, magnesium-containing pigment is essential to this process; it is generally present in plant leaves, and often in other plant parts as well.

Plants rely on soil primarily for support and water (in quantitative terms), but also obtain compounds of nitrogen, phosphorus, and other crucial elemental nutrients. For the majority of plants to grow successfully they also require oxygen in the atmosphere and around their roots for respiration. However, some plants grow as submerged aquatics, using oxygen dissolved in the surrounding water, and a few specialized vascular plants, such as mangroves, can grow with their roots in anoxic conditions.

Factors Affecting Growth

The genotype of a plant affects its growth, for example selected varieties of wheat grow rapidly, maturing within 110 days, whereas others, in the same environmental conditions, grow more slowly and mature within 155 days.

Growth is also determined by environmental factors, such as temperature, available water, available light, and available nutrients in the soil. Any change in the availability of these external conditions will be reflected in the plants growth.

Biotic factors (living organisms) also affect plant growth.

- Plants compete with other plants for space, water, light and nutrients. Plants can be so crowded that no single individual makes normal growth.
- Many plants rely on birds and insects to effect pollination.
- Grazing animals may affect vegetation.
- Soil fertility is influenced by the activity of bacteria and fungi.
- Bacteria, fungi, viruses, nematodes and insects can parasitise plants.
- Some plant roots require an association with fungi to maintain normal activity (mycorrhizal association).

Simple plants like algae may have short life spans as individuals, but their populations are commonly seasonal. Other plants may be organized according to their seasonal growth pattern.

Among the vascular plants, perennials include both evergreens that keep their leaves the entire year, and deciduous plants which lose their leaves for some part of it. In temperate and boreal climates, they generally lose their leaves during the winter; many tropical plants lose their leaves during the dry season.

The growth rate of plants is extremely variable. Some mosses grow less than 0.001 mm/h, while most trees grow 0.025-0.250 mm/h. Some climbing species, such as kudzu, which do not need to produce thick supportive tissue, may grow up to 12.5 mm/h.

Plants protect themselves from frost and dehydration stress with antifreeze proteins, heat-shock proteins and sugars (sucrose is common). LEA (Late Embryogenesis Abundant) protein expression is induced by stresses and protects other proteins from aggregation as a result of desiccation and freezing.

Internal Distribution

Vascular plants differ from other plants in that they transport nutrients between different parts through specialized structures, called xylem and phloem. They also have roots for taking up water and minerals. The xylem moves water and minerals from the root to the rest of the plant, and the phloem provides the roots with sugars and other nutrient produced by the leaves.

Ecology

The photosynthesis conducted by land plants and algae is the ultimate source of energy and organic material in nearly all ecosystems. Photosynthesis radically changed the composition of the early Earth's atmosphere, which as a result is now 21% oxygen. Animals and most other organisms are aerobic, relying on oxygen; those that do not are confined to relatively rare anaerobic environments. Plants are the primary producers in most terrestrial ecosystems and form the basis of the food web in those ecosystems. Many animals rely on plants for shelter as well as oxygen and food.

Land plants are key components of the water cycle and several other biogeochemical cycles. Some plants have coevolved with nitrogen fixing bacteria, making plants an important part of the nitrogen cycle. Plant roots play an essential role in soil development and prevention of soil erosion.

Distribution

Plants are distributed worldwide in varying numbers. While they inhabit a multitude of biomes and ecoregions, few can be found beyond the tundras at the northernmost regions of continental shelves. At the southern extremes, plants have adapted tenaciously to the prevailing conditions.

Plants are often the dominant physical and structural component of habitats where they occur. Many of the Earth's biomes are named for the type of vegetation because plants are the dominant organisms in those biomes, such as grasslands and forests.

Ecological Relationships

Numerous animals have coevolved with plants. Many animals pollinate flowers in exchange for food in the form of pollen or nectar. Many animals disperse seeds, often by eating fruit and passing the seeds in their feces. Myrmecophytes are plants that have coevolved with ants. The plant provides a home, and sometimes food, for the ants. In exchange, the ants defend the plant from herbivores and sometimes competing plants. Ant wastes provide organic fertilizer.

The majority of plant species have various kinds of fungi associated with their root systems in a kind of mutualistic symbiosis known as mycorrhiza. The fungi help the plants gain water and mineral nutrients from the soil, while the plant gives the fungi carbohydrates manufactured in photosynthesis. Some plants serve as homes for endophytic fungi that protect the plant from herbivores by producing toxins. The fungal endophyte, *Neotyphodium coenophialum*, in tall fescue (*Festuca arundinacea*) does tremendous economic damage to the cattle industry in the U.S.

Various forms of parasitism are also fairly common among plants, from the semi-parasitic mistletoe that merely takes some nutrients from its host, but still has photosynthetic leaves, to the fully parasitic broomrape and toothwort that acquire all their nutrients through connections to the roots of other plants, and so have no chlorophyll. Some plants, known as myco-heterotrophs, parasitize mycorrhizal fungi, and hence act as epiparasites on other plants.

Many plants are epiphytes, meaning they grow on other plants, usually trees, without parasitizing them. Epiphytes may indirectly harm their host plant by intercepting mineral nutrients and light that the host would otherwise receive. The weight of large numbers of epiphytes may break tree limbs. Many orchids, bromeliads, ferns and mosses often grow as epiphytes. Bromeliad epiphytes accumulate water in leaf axils to form phytotelmata, complex aquatic food webs.

A few plants are carnivorous, such as the Venus flytrap and sundew. They trap small animals and digest them to obtain mineral nutrients, especially nitrogen.

Importance

The study of plant uses by people is termed economic botany or ethnobotany; some consider economic botany to focus on modern cultivated plants, while ethnobotany focuses on indigenous plants cultivated and used by native peoples. Human cultivation of plants is part of agriculture, which is the basis of human civilization. Plant agriculture is subdivided into agronomy, horticulture and forestry.

Food

Much of human nutrition depends on land plants, either directly or indirectly. Human nutrition depends to a large extent on cereals, especially maize (or corn), wheat and rice. Other staple crops include potato, cassava, and legumes. Human food also includes vegetables, spices, and certain fruits, nuts, herbs, and edible flowers. Beverages produced from plants include coffee, tea, wine, beer and alcohol. Sugar is obtained mainly from sugar cane and sugar beet. Cooking oils and margarine come from maize, soybean, rapeseed, safflower, sunflower, olive and others. Food additives include gum arabic, guar gum, locust bean gum, starch and pectin. Livestock animals including cows, pigs, sheep, and goats are all herbivores; and feed primarily or entirely on cereal plants, particularly grasses.

Non-food Products

Wood is used for buildings, furniture, paper, cardboard, musical instruments and sports equipment. Cloth is often made from cotton, flax or synthetic fibers derived from cellulose, such as rayon and acetate. Renewable fuels from plants include firewood, peat and many other biofuels. Coal and petroleum are fossil fuels derived from plants. Medicines derived from plants include aspirin, taxol, morphine, quinine, reserpine, colchicine, digitalis and vincristine. There are hundreds of herbal supplements such as ginkgo, Echinacea, feverfew, and Saint John's wort. Pesticides derived from plants include nicotine, rotenone, strychnine and pyrethrins. Drugs obtained from plants include opium, cocaine and marijuana. Poisons from plants include ricin, hemlock and curare. Plants are the source of many natural products such as fibers, essential oils, dyes, pigments, waxes, tannins, latex, gums, resins, alkaloids, amber and cork. Products derived from plants include soaps, paints, shampoos, perfumes, cosmetics, turpentine, rubber, varnish, lubricants, linoleum, plastics, inks, chewing gum and hemp rope. Plants are also a primary source of basic chemicals for the industrial synthesis of a vast array of organic chemicals. These chemicals are used in a vast variety of studies and experiments.

Aesthetic Uses

Thousands of plant species are cultivated to beautify the human environment as well as to provide shade, modify temperatures, reduce windspeed, abate noise, provide privacy, and prevent soil erosion.

People use cut flowers, dried flowers and house plants indoors. Outdoors, they use lawn grasses, shade trees, ornamental trees, shrubs, vines, herbaceous perennials and bedding plants.

Images of plants are often used in art, architecture, humor, language, and photography; and on textiles, money, stamps, flags and coats of arms. Living plant art forms include topiary, bonsai, ikebana and espalier.

Ornamental plants have sometimes changed the course of history, as in tulipomania.

Plants are the basis of a multi-billion dollar per year tourism industry which includes travel to arboretums, botanical gardens, historic gardens, national parks, tulip festivals, rainforests, forests with colorful autumn leaves and the National Cherry Blossom Festival.

Venus flytrap, sensitive plant and resurrection plant are examples of plants sold as novelties.

Scientific and Cultural Uses

Tree rings are an important method of dating in archeology and serve as a record of past climates. Basic biological research has often been done with plants, such as the pea plants used to derive Gregor Mendel's laws of genetics. Space stations or space colonies may one day rely on plants for life support. Plants are used as national and state emblems, including state trees and state flowers. Ancient trees are revered and many are famous. Numerous world records are held by plants. Plants are often used as memorials, gifts and to mark special occasions such as births, deaths, weddings and holidays. Plants figure prominently in mythology, religion and literature. The field of ethnobotany studies plant use by indigenous cultures which helps to conserve endangered species as well as discover new medicinal plants. Gardening is the most popular leisure activity in the U.S. Working with plants or horticulture therapy is beneficial for rehabilitating people with disabilities. Certain plants contain psychotropic chemicals which are extracted and ingested, including tobacco, cannabis (marijuana), and opium.

Negative Effects

Weeds are plants that grow where people do not want them. People have spread plants beyond their native ranges and some of these introduced plants become invasive, damaging existing ecosystems by displacing native species. Invasive plants cause billions of dollars in crop losses annually by displacing crop plants, they increase the cost of production and the use of chemical means to control them affects the environment.

Plants may cause harm to people. Plants that produce windblown pollen invoke allergic reactions in people who suffer from hay fever. A wide variety of plants are poisonous. Several plants cause skin irritations when touched, such as poison ivy. Certain plants contain psychotropic chemicals, which are extracted and ingested or smoked, including tobacco, cannabis (marijuana), cocaine and opium, causing damage to health or even death. Both illegal and legal drugs derived from plants have negative effects on the economy, affecting worker productivity and law enforcement costs. Some plants cause allergic reactions in people and animals when ingested, while other plants cause food intolerances that negatively affect health.

Plant Physiology

Plant physiology is a subdiscipline of botany concerned with the function, or physiology, of plants. Closely related fields include plant morphology (structure of plants), plant ecology (interactions with the environment), phytochemistry (biochemistry of plants), cell biology, and molecular biology.

Fundamental processes such as photosynthesis, respiration, plant nutrition, plant hormone functions, tropisms, nastic movements, photoperiodism, photomorphogenesis, circadian rhythms, environmental stress physiology, seed germination, dormancy and stomata function and transpiration, both part of plant water relations, are studied by plant physiologists.

Scope

The field of plant physiology includes the study of all the internal activities of plants—those chemical and physical processes associated with life as they occur in plants. This includes study at many levels of scale of size and time. At the smallest scale are molecular interactions of photosynthesis and internal diffusion of water, minerals, and nutrients. At the largest scale are the processes of plant development, seasonality, dormancy, and reproductive control. Major subdisciplines of plant physiology include phytochemistry (the study of the biochemistry of plants) and phytopathology (the study of disease in plants). The scope of plant physiology as a discipline may be divided into several major areas of research.

First, the study of phytochemistry (plant chemistry) is included within the domain of plant physiology. In order to function and survive, plants produce a wide array of chemical compounds not found in other organisms. Photosynthesis requires a large array of pigments, enzymes, and other compounds to function. Because they cannot move, plants must also defend themselves chemically from herbivores, pathogens and competition from other plants. They do this by producing toxins and foul-tasting or smelling chemicals. Other compounds defend plants against disease, permit survival during drought, and prepare plants for dormancy. While other compounds are used to attract pollinators or herbivores to spread ripe seeds.

Secondly, plant physiology includes the study of biological and chemical processes of individual plant cells. Plant cells have a number of features that distinguish them from cells of animals, and which lead to major differences in the way that plant life behaves and responds differently from animal life. For example, plant cells have a cell wall which restricts the shape of plant cells and thereby limits the flexibility and mobility of plants. Plant cells also contain chlorophyll, a chemical compound that interacts with light in a way that enables plants to manufacture their own nutrients rather than consuming other living things as animals do.

Thirdly, plant physiology deals with interactions between cells, tissues, and organs within a plant. Different cells and tissues are physically and chemically specialized to perform different functions. Roots and rhizoids function to anchor the plant and acquire minerals in the soil. Leaves function to catch light in order to manufacture nutrients. For both of these organs to remain living, the minerals acquired by the roots must be transported to the leaves and the nutrients manufactured in the leaves must be transported to the roots. Plants have developed a number of means by which this transport may occur, such as vascular tissue, and the functioning of the various modes of transport is studied by plant physiologists.

Fourthly, plant physiologists study the ways that plants control or regulate internal functions. Like animals, plants produce chemicals called hormones which are produced in one part of the plant to signal cells in another part of the plant to respond. Many flowering plants bloom at the appropriate time because of light-sensitive compounds that respond to the length of the night, a phenomenon known as photoperiodism. The ripening of fruit and loss of leaves in the winter are controlled in part by the production of the gas ethylene by the plant.

Finally, plant physiology includes the study of how plants respond to conditions and variation in the environment, a field known as environmental physiology. Stress from water loss, changes in air chemistry, or crowding by other plants can lead to changes in the way a plant functions. These changes may be affected by genetic, chemical, and physical factors.

Biochemistry of Plants

The list of simple elements of which plants are primarily constructed—carbon, oxygen, hydrogen, calcium, phosphorus, etc.—is not different from similar lists for animals, fungi, or even bacteria. The fundamental atomic components of plants are the same as for all life; only the details of the way in which they are assembled differs.

Despite this underlying similarity, plants produce a vast array of chemical compounds with unusual properties which they use to cope with their environment. Pigments are used by plants to absorb or detect light, and are extracted by humans for use in dyes. Other plant products may be used for the manufacture of commercially important rubber or biofuel. Perhaps the most celebrated compounds from plants are those with pharmacological activity, such as salicylic acid (aspirin), morphine, and digitalis. Drug companies spend billions of dollars each year researching plant compounds for potential medicinal benefits.

Constituent Elements

Plants require some nutrients, such as carbon and nitrogen, in large quantities to survive. Such nutrients are termed macronutrients, where the prefix *macro-* (large) refers to the quantity needed, not the size of the nutrient particles themselves. Other nutrients, called micronutrients, are required only in trace amounts for plants to remain healthy. Such micronutrients are usually absorbed as ions dissolved in water taken from the soil, though carnivorous plants acquire some of their micronutrients from captured prey.

The following Table 2.1 list element nutrients essential to plants. Uses within plants are generalized.

Table 2.1: List of element nutrients essential to plans

Micronutrients (Necessary in large quantities)

Element	Form of uptake	Notes
Nitrogen	NO_3^-, NH_4^+	Nucleic acids, proteins, hormones, etc.
Oxygen	O_2H_2O	Cellulose, starch, other organic compounds
Carbon	CO_2	Cellulose, starch, other organic compounds
Hydrogen	H_2O	Cellulose, starch, other organic compounds

(Contd...)

Potassium	K^+	Cofactor in protein synthesis, water balance, etc.
Calcium	Ca^{2+}	Membrane synthesis and stabilization
Magnesium	Mg^{2+}	Element essential for chlorophyll
Phosphorus	H_2PO_4	Nucleic acids, phospholipids, ATP
Sulfur	SO_4^{2-}	Constituent of proteins and coenzymes

Micronutrients (Necessary in small quantities)

Element	Form of uptake	Notes
Chlorine	Cl^-	Photosystem II and stomata function
Iron	Fe^{2+}, Fe^{3+}	Chorophyll formation
Boron	HBO_3	Crosslinking pectin
Manganese	Mn^{2+}	Activity of some enzymes
Zinc	Zn^{2+}	Involved in the synthesis of enzymes and chlorophyll
Copper	Cu^+	Enzymes for lignin synthesis
Molybdenum	MoO_4^{2-}	Nitrogen fixation, reduction of nitrates
Nickel	Ni^{2+}	Enzymatic cofactor in the metabolism of nitrogen compounds

Pigments

Among the most important molecules for plant function are the pigments. Plant pigments include a variety of different kinds of molecules, including porphyrins, carotenoids, and anthocyanins. All biological pigments selectively absorb certain wavelengths of light while reflecting others. The light that is absorbed may be used by the plant to power chemical reactions, while the reflected wavelengths of light determine the color the pigment will appear to the eye.

Chlorophyll is the primary pigment in plants; it is a porphyrin that absorbs red and blue wavelengths of light while reflecting green. It is the presence and relative abundance of chlorophyll that gives plants their green color. All land plants and green algae possess two forms of this pigment: chlorophyll *a* and chlorophyll *b*. Kelps, diatoms, and other photosynthetic heterokonts contain chlorophyll *c* instead of *b*, while red algae possess only chlorophyll *a*. All chlorophylls serve as the primary means plants use to intercept light in order to fuel photosynthesis.

Carotenoids are red, orange, or yellow tetraterpenoids. They function as accessory pigments in plants, helping to fuel photosynthesis by gathering wavelengths of light not readily absorbed by chlorophyll. The most familiar carotenoids are carotene (an orange pigment found in carrots), lutein (a yellow pigment found in fruits and vegetables), and lycopene (the red pigment responsible for the color of tomatoes). Carotenoids have been shown to act as antioxidants and to promote healthy eyesight in humans.

Anthocyanins (literally "flower blue") are water-soluble flavonoid pigments that appear red to blue, according to pH. They occur in all tissues of higher plants, providing color in leaves, stems, roots, flowers, and fruits, though not always in sufficient quantities to be noticeable. Anthocyanins are most visible in the petals of flowers, where they may make up as much as 30% of the dry weight of the tissue. They are also responsible for the purple color seen on the underside of tropical shade plants such as *Tradescantia zebrina*; in these plants, the anthocyanin catches light that has passed through the leaf and reflects it back towards regions bearing chlorophyll, in order to maximize the use of available light.

Betalains are red or yellow pigments. Like anthocyanins they are water-soluble, but unlike anthocyanins they are indole-derived compounds synthesized from tyrosine. This class of pigments is found only in the Caryophyllales (including cactus and amaranth), and never co-occur in plants with anthocyanins. Betalains are responsible for the deep red color of beets, and are used commercially as food-coloring agents. Plant physiologists are uncertain of the function that betalains have in plants which possess them, but there is some preliminary evidence that they may have fungicidal properties.

Signals and Regulators

Plants produce hormones and other growth regulators which act to signal a physiological response in their tissues. They also produce compounds such as phytochrome that are sensitive to light and which serve to trigger growth or development in response to environmental signals.

Plant Hormones

Plant hormones, also known as plant growth regulators (PGRs) or phytohormones, are chemicals that regulate a plant's growth. According to a standard animal definition, hormones are signal molecules produced at specific locations, that occur in very low concentrations, and cause altered processes in target cells at other locations. Unlike animals, plants lack specific hormone-producing tissues or organs. Plant hormones are often not transported to other parts of the plant and production is not limited to specific locations.

Plant hormones are chemicals that in small amounts promote and influence the growth, development and differentiation of cells and tissues. Hormones are vital to plant growth; affecting processes in plants from flowering to seed development, dormancy, and germination. They regulate which tissues grow upwards and which grow downwards, leaf formation and stem growth, fruit development and ripening, as well as leaf abscission and even plant death.

The most important plant hormones are abscissic acid (ABA), auxins, gibberellins, and cytokinins, though there are many other substances that serve to regulate plant physiology.

Photomorphogenesis

While most people know that light is important for photosynthesis in plants, few realize that plant sensitivity to light plays a role in the control of plant structural development (morphogenesis). The use of light to control structural development is called photomorphogenesis, and is dependent upon the presence of specialized photoreceptors, which are chemical pigments capable of absorbing specific wavelengths of light.

Plants use four kinds of photoreceptors phytochrome, cryptochrome, a UV-B photoreceptor, and protochlorophyllide *a*. The first two of these, phytochrome and cryptochrome, are photoreceptor proteins, complex molecular structures formed by joining a protein with a light-sensitive pigment. Cryptochrome is also known as the UV-A photoreceptor, because it absorbs ultraviolet light in the long wave "A" region. The UV-B receptor is one or more compounds that have yet to be identified with certainty, though some evidence suggests carotene or riboflavin as candidates Protochlorophyllide *a*, as its name suggests, is a chemical precursor of chlorophyll.

The most studied of the photoreceptors in plants is phytochrome. It is sensitive to light in the red and far-red region of the visible spectrum. Many flowering plants use it to regulate the time of flowering based on the length of day and night (photoperiodism) and to set circadian rhythms. It also regulates other responses including the germination of seeds, elongation of seedlings, the size, shape and number of leaves, the synthesis of chlorophyll, and the straightening of the epicotyl or hypocotyl hook of dicot seedlings.

Photoperiodism

Many flowering plants use the pigment phytochrome to sense seasonal changes in day length, which they take as signals to flower. This sensitivity to day length is termed photoperiodism. Broadly speaking, flowering plants can be classified as long day plants, short day plants, or day neutral plants, depending on their particular response to changes in day length. Long day plants require a certain minimum length of daylight to initiate flowering, so these plants flower in the spring or summer. Conversely, short day plants will flower when the length of daylight falls below a certain critical level. Day neutral plants do not initiate flowering based on photoperiodism, though some may use temperature sensitivity (vernalization) instead.

Although a short day plant cannot flower during the long days of summer, it is not actually the period of light exposure that limits flowering. Rather, a short day plant requires a minimal length of uninterrupted darkness in each 24 hour period (a short daylength) before floral development can begin. It has been determined experimentally that a short day plant (long night) will not flower if a flash of phytochrome activating light is used on the plant during the night.

Plants make use of the phytochrome system to sense day length or photoperiod. This fact is utilized by florists and greenhouse gardeners to control and even induce flowering out of season, such as the *Poinsettia*.

Environmental Physiology

Paradoxically, the subdiscipline of environmental physiology is on the one hand a recent field of study in plant ecology and on the other hand one of the oldest Environmental philology is the preferred name of the subdiscipline among plant physiologists, but it goes by a number of other names in the applied sciences. It is roughly synonymous with ecophysiology, crop ecology, horticulture, and agronomy. The particular name applied to the subdiscipline is specific to the viewpoint and goals of research. Whatever name is applied, it deals with the ways in which plants respond to their environment and so overlaps with the field of ecology.

Environmental physiologists examine plant response to physical factors such as radiation (including light and ultraviolet radiation), temperature, fire, and wind. Of particular importance are water relations (which can be measured with the Pressure bomb) and the stress of drought or inundation, exchange of gases with the atmosphere, as well as the cycling of nutrients such as nitrogen and carbon.

Environmental physiologists also examine plant response to biological factors. This includes not only negative interactions, such as competition, herbivory, disease, and parasitism, but also positive interactions, such as mutualism and pollination.

Tropisms and Nastic Movements

Plants may respond both to directional and nondirectional stimuli. A response to a directional stimulus, such as gravity or sunlight, is called a tropism. A response to a nondirectional stimulus, such as temperature or humidity, is a nastic movement.

Tropisms in plants are the result of differential cell growth, in which the cells on one side of the plant elongate more than those on the other side, causing the part to bend toward the side with less growth. Among the common tropisms seen in plants is phototropism, the bending of the plant toward a source of light. Phototropism allows the plant to maximize light exposure in plants which require additional light for photosynthesis, or to minimize it in plants subjected to intense light and heat. Geotropism allows the roots of a plant to determine the direction of gravity and grow downwards. Tropisms generally result from an interaction between the environment and production of one or more plant hormones.

In contrast to tropisms, nastic movements result from changes in turgor pressure within plant tissues, and may occur rapidly. A familiar example is thigmonasty (response to touch) in the Venus fly trap, a carnivorous plant. The traps consist of modified leaf blades which bear sensitive trigger hairs. When the hairs are touched by an insect or other animal, the leaf folds shut. This mechanism allows the plant to trap and digest small insects for additional nutrients. Although the trap is rapidly shut by changes in internal cell pressures, the leaf must grow slowly in order to reset for a second opportunity to trap insects.

Plant Disease

Economically, one of the most important areas of research in environmental physiology is that of phytopathology, the study of diseases in plants and the manner in which plants resist or cope with infection. Plant are susceptible to the same kinds of disease organisms as animals, including viruses, bacteria, and fungi, as well as physical invasion by insects and roundworms.

Because the biology of plants differs from animals, their symptoms and responses are quite different. In some cases, a plant can simply shed infected leaves or flowers to prevent to spread of disease, in a process called abscission. Most animals do not have this option as a means of controlling disease. Plant diseases organisms themselves also differ from those causing disease in animals because plants cannot usually spread infection through casual physical contact. Plant pathogens tend to spread via spores or are carried by animal vectors.

One of the most important advances in the control of plant disease was the discovery of Bordeaux mixture in the nineteenth century. The mixture is the first known fungicide and is a combination of copper sulfate and lime. Application of the mixture served to inhibit the growth of downy mildew that threatened to seriously damage the French wine industry.

History

Early Research

Sir Francis Bacon published one of the first plant physiology experiments in 1627 in the book, *Sylva Sylvarum.* Bacon grew several terrestrial plants, including a rose, in water and concluded that soil was only needed to keep the plant upright. Jan Baptist van Helmont published what is considered the first quantitative experiment in plant physiology in 1648. He grew a willow tree for five years in a pot containing 200 pounds of oven-dry soil. The soil lost just two ounces of dry weight and van Helmont concluded that plants get all their weight from water, not soil. In 1699, John Woodward published experiments on growth of spearmint in different sources of water. He found that plants grew much better in water with soil added than in distilled water.

Stephen Hales is considered the Father of Plant Physiology for the many experiments in the 1727 book though Julius von Sachs unified the pieces of plant physiology and put them together as a discipline. His *Lehrbuch der Botanik* was the plant physiology bible of its time.

Researchers discovered in the 1800s that plants absorb essential mineral nutrients as inorganic ions in water. In natural conditions, soil acts as a mineral nutrient reservoir but the soil itself is not essential to plant growth. When the mineral nutrients in the soil are dissolved in water, plant roots absorb nutrients readily, soil is no longer required for the plant to thrive. This observation is the basis for hydroponics, the growing of plants in a water solution rather than soil, which has become a standard technique in biological research, teaching lab exercises, crop production and as a hobby.

Current Research

One of the leading journals in the field is *Plant Physiology*, started in 1926. All its back issues are available online for free. Many other journals often carry plant physiology articles, including *Physiologia Plantarum*, *Journal of Experimental Botany*, *American Journal of Botany*, *Annals of Botany*, *Journal of Plant Nutrition* and *Proceedings of the National Academy of Sciences.*

Economic Applications

Food Production

In horticulture and agriculture along with food science, plant physiology is an important topic relating to fruits, vegetables, and other consumable parts of plants. Topics studied include: *climatic* requirements, fruit drop, nutrition, ripening, fruit set. The production of food crops also hinges on the study of plant physiology covering such topics as Optimal planting and harvesting times and post harvest storage of plant products for human consumption and the production of secondary products like drugs and cosmetics.

CHAPTER

3

Plant Morphology

Plant morphology (or phytomorphology) is the general term for the study of the morphology (physical form and external structure) of plants. This is usually considered distinct from plant anatomy, which is the study of the internal structure of plants, especially at the microscopic level. Plant morphology is useful in the identification of plants.

Scope

Plant morphology "represents a study of the development, form, and structure of plants, and, by implication, an attempt to interpret these on the basis of similarity of plan and origin. There are four major areas of investigation in plant morphology, and each overlaps with another field of the biological sciences.

First of all, morphology is comparative, meaning that the morphologist examines structures in many different plants of the same or different species, then draws comparisons and formulates ideas about similarities. When structures in different species are believed to exist and develop as a result of common, inherited genetic pathways, those structures are termed homologous. For example, the leaves of pine, oak, and cabbage all look very different, but share certain basic structures and arrangement of parts. The homology of leaves is an easy conclusion to make. The plant morphologist goes further, and discovers that the spines of cactus also share the same basic structure and development as leaves in other plants, and therefore cactus spines are homologous to leaves as well. This aspect of plant morphology overlaps with the study of plant evolution and paleobotany.

Secondly, plant morphology observes both the vegetative (somatic) structures of plants, as well as the reproductive structures. The vegetative structures of vascular plants includes the study of the shoot system, composed of stems and leaves, as well as the root system. The reproductive structures are more varied, and are usually specific to a particular group of plants, such as flowers and seeds, fern sori, and moss capsules. The detailed study of reproductive structures in plants led to the discovery of the alternation of generations found in all plants and most algae. This area of plant morphology overlaps with the study of biodiversity and plant systematics.

Thirdly, plant morphology studies plant structure at a range of scales. At the smallest scales are ultrastructure, the general structural features of cells visible only with the aid of an electron microscope, and cytology, the study of cells using optical microscopy. At this scale, plant morphology overlaps with plant anatomy as a field of study. At the largest scale is the study of plant growth habit, the overall architecture of a plant. The pattern of branching in a tree will vary from species to species, as will the appearance of a plant as a tree, herb, or grass.

Fourthly, plant morphology examines the pattern of development, the process by which structures originate and mature as a plant grows. While animals produce all the body parts they will ever have from early in their life, plants constantly produce new tissues and structures throughout their life. A living plant always has embryonic tissues. The way in which new structures mature as they are produced may be affected by the point in the plants life when they begin to develop, as well as by the environment to which the structures are exposed. A morphologist studies this process, the causes, and its result. This area of plant morphology overlaps with plant physiology and ecology.

A Comparative Science

A plant morphologist makes comparisons between structures in many different plants of the same or different species. Making such comparisons between similar structures in different plants tackles the question of *why* the structures are similar. It is quite likely that similar underlying causes of genetics, physiology, or response to the environment have led to this similarity in appearance. The result of scientific investigation into these causes can lead to one of two insights into the underlying biology:

- **Homology** - the structure is similar between the two species because of shared ancestry and common genetics.
- **Convergence** - the structure is similar between the two species because of independent adaptation to common environmental pressures.

Understanding which characteristics and structures belong to each type is an important part of understanding plant evolution. The evolutionary biologist relies on the plant morphologist to interpret structures, and in turn provides phylogenies of plant relationships that may lead to new morphological insights.

Homology

When structures in different species are believed to exist and develop as a result of common, inherited genetic pathways, those structures are termed *homologous*. For example, the leaves of pine, oak, and cabbage all look very different, but share certain basic structures and arrangement of parts. The homology of leaves is an easy conclusion to make. The plant morphologist goes further, and discovers that the spines of cactus also share the same basic structure and development as leaves in other plants, and therefore cactus spines are homologous to leaves as well.

Convergence

When structures in different species are believed to exist and develop as a result of common adaptive responses to environmental pressure, those structures are termed *convergent*. For example, the fronds of *Bryopsis plumosa* and stems of *Asparagus setaceus* both have the same feathery branching appearance, even though one is an alga and one is a flowering plant. The similarity in overall structure occurs independently as a result of convergence. The growth form of many cacti and species of *Euphorbia* is very similar, even though they belong to widely distant families. The similarity results from common solutions to the problem of surviving in a hot, dry environment.

Vegetative and Reproductive Characters

Plant morphology treats both the vegetative structures of plants, as well as the reproductive structures.

The vegetative (somatic) structures of vascular plants include two major organ systems:

1. a *shoot system*, composed of stems and leaves; and
2. a *root system*.

These two systems are common to nearly all vascular plants, and provide a unifying theme for the study of plant morphology.

By contrast, the reproductive structures are varied, and are usually specific to a particular group of plants.

Structures such as flowers and fruits are only found in the angiosperms; sori are only found in ferns; and seed cones are only found in conifers and other gymnosperms. Reproductive characters are therefore regarded as more useful for the classification of plants than vegetative characters.

Use in Identification

Plant biologists use morphological characters of plants which can be compared, measured counted and described to assess the differences or similarities in plant taxa and use these characters for plant identification, classification and descriptions. When characters are used in descriptions or for identification they are called *diagnostic* or *key characters* which can be either qualitative and quantitative.

1. Quantitative characters are morphological features that can be counted or measured for example a plant species has flower petals 10-12 mm wide.
2. Qualitative characters are morphological features such as leaf shape, flower color or pubescence.

Both kinds of characters can be very useful for the identification of plants.

Alternation of Generations

The detailed study of reproductive structures in plants led to the discovery of the alternation of generations, found in all plants and most algae, by the German botanist Wilhelm Hofmeister. This discovery is one of the most important made in all of plant morphology, since it provides a common basis for understanding the life cycle of all plants.

Plant Development

Plant development is the process by which structures originate and mature as a plant grows. It is a subject studies in plant anatomy and plant physiology as well as plant morphology.

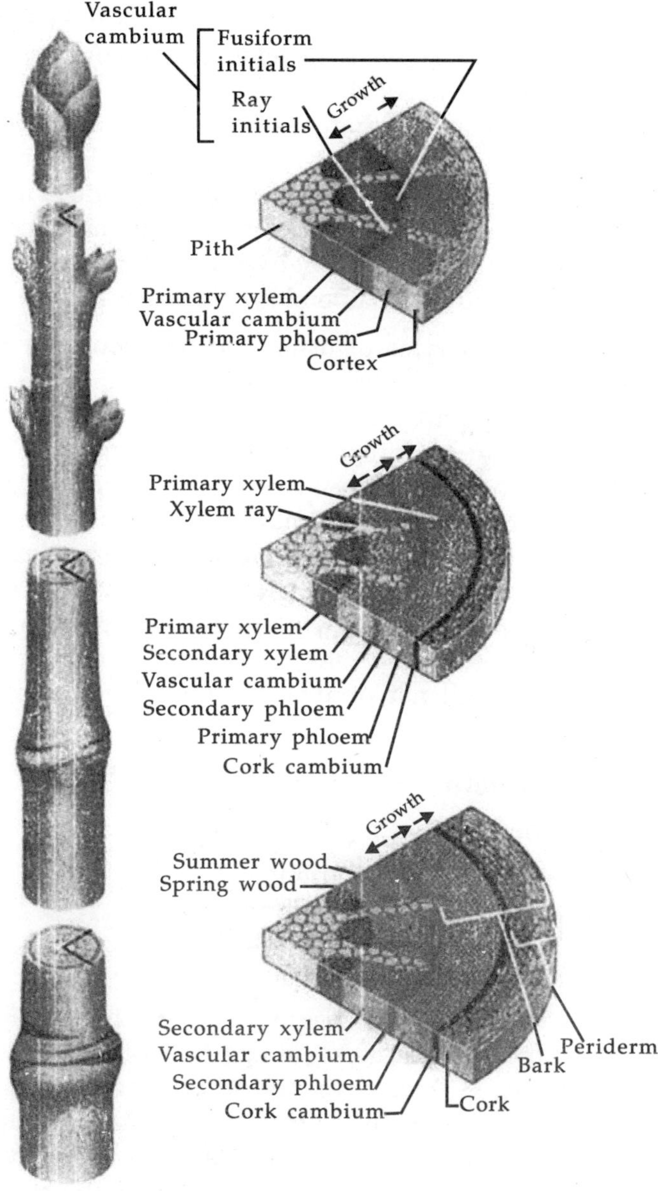

Fig. 3.1: **Plant development progressive sections of a stem**

The process of development in plants is fundamentally different from that seen in vertebrate animals. When an animal embryo begins to develop, it will very early produce all of the body parts that will ever have in its life. When the animal is born. or hatches from its egg. it has all its body parts and from that point will only grow larger and more mature. By contrast, plants constantly produce new tissues and structures throughout their life from meristems located at the tips of organs, or between mature tissues. Thus, a living plant always has embryonic tissues.

The properties of organization seen in a plant are emergent properties which are more than the sum of the individual parts. "The assembly of these tissues and functions into an integrated multicellular organism yields not only the characteristics of the separate parts and processes but also quite a new set of characteristics which would not have been predictable on the basis of examination of the separate parts." In other words, knowing everything about the molecules in a plant are not enough to predict characteristics of the cells; and knowing all the properties of the cells will not predict all the properties of a plant's structure.

Plant Growth

- Meristem;
- Cellular differentiation;
- Morphogenesis; and
- Plant embryogenesis.

A vascular plant begins from a single celled zygote, formed by fertilisation of an egg cell by a sperm cell. From that point, it begins to divide to form a plant embryo through the process of embryogenesis. As this happens, the resulting cells will organize so that one end becomes the first root, while the other end forms the tip of the shoot. In seed plants, the embryo will develop one or more "seed leaves" (cotyledons). By the end of embryogenesis, the young plant will have all the parts necessary to begin in its life.

Once the embryo germinates from its seed or parent plant, it begins to produce additional organs (leaves, stems, and roots) through the process of organogenesis. New roots grow from root meristems located at the tip of the root, and new stems and leaves grow from shoot meristems located at the tip of the shoot. Branching occurs when small clumps of cells left behind by the meristem, and which have not yet undergone cellular differentiation to form a specialized tissue, begin to grow as the tip of a new root or shoot. Growth from any such meristem at the tip of a root or shoot is termed primary growth and results in the lengthening of that root or shoot. Secondary growth results in widening of a root or shoot from divisions of cells in a cambium.

In addition to growth by cell division, a plant may grow through cell elongation. This occurs when individual cells or groups of cells grow longer. Not all plant cells will grow to the same length. When cells on one side of a stem grow longer and faster than cells on the other side, the stem will bend to the side of the slower growing cells as a result.

Morphological Variation

Plants exhibit natural variation in their form and structure. While all organisms vary from individual to individual, plants exhibit an additional type of variation. Within a single individual, parts are repeated which may differ in form and structure from other similar parts. This variation is most easily seen in the leaves of a plant, though other organs such as stems and flowers may show similar variation. There are three primary causes of this variation: positional effects, environmental effects, and juvenility.

Positional Effects

Although plants produce numerous copies of the same organ during their lives, not all copies of a particular organ will be identical. There is variation among the parts of a mature plant resulting from the relative position where the organ is produced. For example, along a new branch the leaves may vary in a consistent pattern along the branch. The form of leaves produced near the base of the branch will differ from leaves produced at the tip of the plant, and this difference is consistent from branch to branch on a given plant and in a given species. This difference persists after the leaves at both ends of the branch have matured, and is not the result of some leaves being younger than others.

Environmental Effects

The way in which new structures mature as they are produced may be affected by the point in the plants life when they begin to develop, as well as by the environment to which the structures are exposed. This can be seen in aquatic plants and emergent plants.

Juvenility

The organs and tissues produced by a young plant, such as a seedling, are often different from those that produced by the same plant when it is older. This phenomenon is known as juvenility. For example, young trees will produce longer, leaner branches that grow upwards more than the branches they will produce as a fully grown tree. In addition, leaves produced during early growth tend to be larger, thinner, and more irregular than leaves on the adult plant. Species of juvenile plants may look so completely different from the adult leaves that egg-laying insects do not recognize the plant as food for their young.

PLANT ANATOMY

Plant Anatomy or phytotomy is the general term for the study of the internal structure of plants. While originally it included plant morphology, which is the description of the physical form and external structure of plants, since the mid Twentieth Century the investigation of plant anatomy is considered a separate, distinct field, and refers to just the internal plant structures. Plant anatomy is now frequently investigated at the cellular level, and often involves the sectioning of tissues and microscopy.

Structural Divisions

Plant anatomy is sometimes divided into the following categories:

- Flower anatomy
  - Calyx
  - Corolla
  - Androecium
  - Gynoecium
- Leaf anatomy
  - Leaf anatomy
- Stem anatomy
  - Stem structure
- Fruit/Seed anatomy
  - Ovule
    - Seed structure
  - Pericarp
  - Accessory fruit
- Wood anatomy
  - Bark
    - Cork
    - Phloem
    - Vascular cambium

Heartwood and sapwood

branch collar

Root anatomy

Root structure

History

About 300 BCE Theophrastus wrote a number of plant treatises, only two of which survive. He developed concepts of plant morphology and classification, which did not withstand the scientific scrutiny of the Renaissance.

A Swiss physician and botanist, Gaspard Bauhin, introduced binomial nomenclature into plant taxonomy. He published *Pinax theatri botanici* in 1596, which was the first to use this convention for naming of species. His criteria for classification included natural relationships, or 'affinities', which in many cases were structural.

Italian doctor and microscopist, Marcello Malpighi, was one of the two founders of plant anatomy. In 1671 he published his *Anatomia Plantarum*, the first major advance in plant physiogamy since Aristotle.

The British doctor, Nehemiah Grew was one of the two founders of plant anatomy. He published *An Idea of a Philosophical History of Plants* in 1672 and *The Anatomy of Plants* in 1682. Grew is credited with the recognition of plant cells, although he called them 'vesicles' and 'bladders'. He correctly identified and described the sexual organs of plants (flowers) and their parts.

In the Eighteenth Century, Carolus Linnaeus established taxonomy based on structure, and his early work was with plant anatomy. While the exact structural level which is to be considered to be scientifically valid for comparison and differentiation has changed with the growth of knowledge, the basic principles were established by Linnaeus. He published his master work, *Species Plantarum* in 1753.

In 1802, French botanist, Charles-François Brisseau de Mirbel, published *Traité d'anatomie et de physiologie végétale* (*Treatise on Plant Anatomy and Physiology*) establishing the beginnings of the science of plant cytology.

In 1812, Johann Jacob Paul Moldenhawer published *Beyträge zur Anatomie der Pflanzen*, describing microscopic studies of plant tissues.

In 1813 a Swiss botanist, Augustin Pyrame de Candolle, published *Théorie élémentaire de la botanique*, in which he argued that plant anatomy, not physiology, ought to be the sole basis for plant classification. Using a scientific basis, he established structural criteria for defining and separating plant genera.

In 1830, Franz Meyen published *Phytotomie*, the first comprehensive review of plant anatomy.

In 1838 German botanist, Matthias Jakob Schleiden, published *Contributions to Phytogenesis*, stating, "the lower plants all consist of one cell, while the higher plants are composed of (many) individual cells" thus confirming and continuing Mirabel's work.

A German-Polish botanist, Eduard Strasburger, described the mitotic process in plant cells and further demonstrated that new cell nuclei can only arise from the division of other pre-existing nuclei. His *Studien über Protoplasma* was published in 1876.

Gottlieb Haberlandt, a German botanist, studied plant physiology and classified plant tissue based upon function. On this basis, in 1884 he published *Physiologische Pflanzenanatomie* (*Physiological Plant Anatomy*) in which he described twelve types of tissue systems (absorptive, mechanical, photosynthetic, etc.).

British paleobotanists Dunkinfield Henry Scott and William Crawford Williamson described the structures of fossilized plants at the end of the Nineteenth Century. Scott's *Studies in Fossil Botany* was published in 1900.

Following Charles Darwin's *Origin of Species* a Canadian botanist, Edward Charles Jeffrey, who was studying the comparative anatomy and phylogeny of different vascular plant groups, applied the theory to plants using the form and structure of plants to establish a number of evolutionary lines. He published his *The Anatomy of Woody Plants* in 1917.

The growth of comparative plant anatomy was spearheaded by a British botanist, Agnes Arber. She published *Water Plants: A Study of Aquatic Angiosperms* in 1920, *Monocotyledons: A Morphological Study* in 1925, and *The Gramineae: A Study of Cereal, Bamboo and Grass* in 1934.

Following World War II, Katherine Esau published, *Plant Anatomy* (1953), which became the definitive textbook on plant structure in North American universities and elsewhere, it was still in print as of 2006. She followed up with her *Anatomy of seed plants* in 1960.

Wood Anatomy

Bark

Bark is the outermost layers of stems and roots of woody plants. Plants with bark include trees, woody vines and shrubs. Bark refers to all the tissues outside of the vascular cambium and is a nontechnical term. It overlays the wood and consists of the inner bark and the outer bark. The inner bark, which in older stems is living tissue, includes the innermost area of the periderm. The outer bark in older stems, includes the dead tissue on the surface of the stems, along with parts of the innermost periderm and all the tissues on the outer side of the periderm. The outer bark on trees is also called the rhytidome. Products used by people that are derived from bark include: spices and other flavorings, tannin, resin, latex, medicines, poisons, various hallucinatory chemicals and cork. Bark has been used to make cloths, canoes, ropes and used as a surface for paintings and map making A number of plants are also grown for their attractive or interesting bark colorations and surface textures.

Botanic Description

Some trees are big, some trees are small, but all trees have bark (except for poplar, ash and maple). What is commonly called bark, includes a number of different tissues. Cork is an external, secondary tissue that is impermeable to water and gases, it is produced by the Cork cambium which is a layer of cells that are in a persistent meristematic state. The cork cambium, which is also called the phellogen, is normally only one or two cell layers thick and the outside surface produces cork. The phelloderm, which is not always present in all barks, is a layer of cells formed from the inner cells of the cork cambium, it contains suberin, a waxy substance which protects the stem against water loss, the invasion of insects into the stem, and prevents infections by bacteria and fungal spores. The cambium tissues are the only parts of a woody stem where cell division occurs; undifferentiated cells in the cambium divide rapidly to produce secondary xylem to the inside and secondary phloem to the outside. Phloem which is a nutrient-conducting tissue composed of sieve tubes or sieve cells mixed with parenchyma and fibers. The Cortex is the primary tissue of stems and roots. In stems the cortex is between the epidermis layer and the phloem, in roots the inner layer is not phloem but the pericycle. From the outside to the inside of a mature woody stem, these layers are arranged:

1. Cork (Phellem)
2. Cork cambium (Phellogen)
3. Phelloderm
4. Cortex
5. Phloem
6. Cambium
7. Xylem.

The bark includes (1) through (5), and is composed of periderm and phloem and the cells that produce these tissues The periderms includes (1),(2) and (3).

In young stems, which lack what is commonly called bark, the tissues are from the outside to the inside: epidermis, periderm, cortex, primary phloem, secondary phloem, vascular cambium and then xylem. As the stem ages and grows, changes occur that transform the surface of the stem into the bark. The epidermis, which is a layer of cells that cover the plant body, including the stems, leaves, flowers and fruits, that protects the plant from the outside world. In old stems the epidermal layer, cortex, and primary phloem become separated from the inner tissues by thicker formations of cork. Due to the thickening cork layer these cells die because they do not receive water and nutrients. This dead layer is the rough corky bark that forms around tree trunks and other stems.

Periderm

In smaller stems and on typically non woody plants, sometimes a secondary covering forms called the periderm, which is composed of cork, the cork cambium, and the phelloderm. It replaces the epidermis, and acts as a protective covering like the epidermis, it too is made up of mostly dead tissue. The skin on the potato is a periderm. In woody plants the epidermis of newly grown stems is replaced by the periderm later in the year. As the stems grow a layer of cells form under the epidermis, called the cork cambium, these cells produce cork cells that turn into cork. The single cell layer of cork cells is called the phelloderm, it is produced inside the cork cambium layer (also called the phellogen). As the stem grows, the phelloderm produces new layers of cork which are impermeable to gases and water and the cells outside of the periderm, namely the epidermis, cortex and older secondary phloem die. As the stem grows wider, the periderm cannot effectively seal the stem from the outside world, thus the formation of cork becomes the new protective surface for the stem.

Within the periderm are lenticels, which form during the production of the first periderm layer. Since there are living cells within the cambium layers that need to exchange gases during metabolism, these lenticels, because they have numerous intercellular spaces, allow gaseous exchange with the outside atmosphere. As the bark develops, new lenticels are formed within the cracks of the cork layers.

Rhytidome

The rhytidome is the most familiar part of bark, it is the outer layer that covers the trunks of trees. It is composed mostly of dead lignified cells and is produced by the formation of multiple layers of periderm tissue. It is generally thickest and most distinctive at the trunk or bole (The area from the ground to where the main branching starts) of the tree.

Uses

Cork, sometimes confused with bark in colloquial speech, is the outermost layer of a woody stem, derived from the cork cambium. It serves as protection against damage from parasites, herbivorous animals and diseases, as well as dehydration and fire. Cork can contain antiseptics like tannins, that protect against fungal and bacterial attacks that would cause decay.

In some plants, the bark is substantially thicker, providing further protection and giving the bark a characteristically distinctive structure with deep ridges. In the cork oak (*Quercus suber*) the bark is thick enough to be harvested as a cork product without killing the tree. Some barks can be removed in long sheets; the smooth surfaced bark of birch trees has been used as a covering in the making of canoes, the most famous example of this is the birch canoes of North America.

The bark of some trees is edible; in Finland, pine bread is made from rye to which the toasted and ground innermost layer of pine bark is added, the Sami people of far northern Europe used large sheets of *Pinus sylvestris* bark that were removed in the spring, prepared and stored for use as a staple food resource and the inner bark was eaten fresh, dried or roasted Bark contains strong fibres known as bast, and there is a long tradition in northern Europe of using bark from coppiced young branches of the small-leaved lime (*Tilia cordata*) to produce cordage and rope, used for example in the rigging of Viking age longships.

Among the commercial products made from bark are cork, cinnamon, quinine (from the bark of Cinchona) and aspirin (from the bark of willow trees). The bark of some trees notably oak (*Quercus robur*) is a source of tannic acid, which is used in tanning. Bark chips generated as a by-product of lumber production, are often used in bark mulch in western North America. Bark is important to the horticultural industry since in shredded form it is used for plants that do not thrive in ordinary soil, such as epiphytes.

Bark Chip Extraction

Wood Adhesives from Bark-Derived Phenols: Wood Bark has lignin content and when it is pyrolyzed (subjected to high temperatures in the absence of oxygen), it yields a liquid bio-oil product rich in natural phenol derivatives. The phenol derivatives are isolated and recovered for application as a replacement for fossil-based phenols in phenol-formaldehyde (PF) resins used in Oriented Strand Board (OSB) and plywood.

Bark Removal

Cut logs used for the production of lumber or even log cabins generally have the bark removed, either just before cutting or for curing. Such logs and even trunks and branches found in their natural state of decay in forests, where the bark has fallen off, are said to be decorticated.

A number of living organisms live in or on bark, including insects, fungi and other plants like mosses , algae and other vascular plants. Many of these organisms are pathogens or parasites but some also have symbiotic relationships.

Bark Repair

The degree to which trees are able to repair gross physical damage to their bark is very variable. Some are able to produce a callus growth which heals over the wound rapidly, but leaves a clear scar, whilst others such as oaks do not produce an extensive callus repair.

Phloem

In vascular plants, phloem is the living tissue that carries organic nutrients (known as photosynthate), particularly sucrose, a sugar, to all parts of the plant where needed. In trees, the phloem is the innermost layer of the bark, hence the name, derived from the Greek word f (*phloos*) "bark". The phloem is mainly concerned with the transport of soluble organic material made during photosynthesis. This is called translocation.

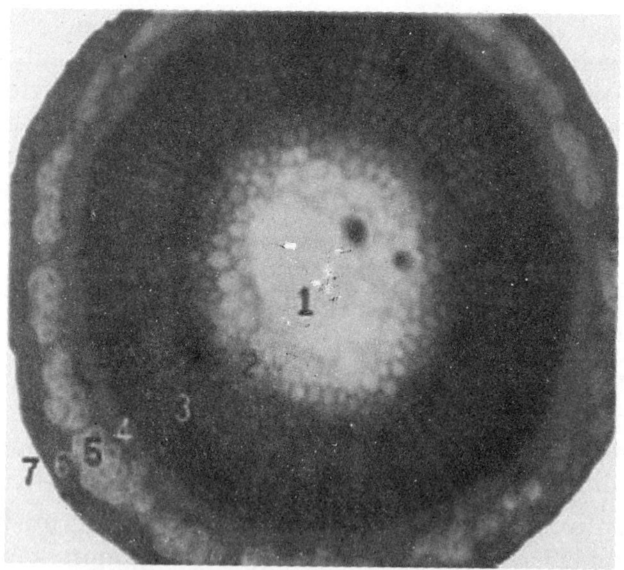

Fig. 4.1: **Cross-section of a flax plant stem: 1. Pith; 2. Protoxylem; 3. Xylem I; 4. Phloem I; 5. Sclerenchyma (bast fibre); 6. Cortex; 7. Epidermis**

Structure

Phloem tissue consists of less specialized and nucleate *parenchyma* cells, *sieve-tube cells,* and *companion cells* (in addition *albuminous* cells, fibres and *sclereids*) (See fig. 3.1).

Phloem tissue con-sists of less specialized and nucleate *paren-chyma* cells, *sieve-tube cells*, and *companion cells* (in addition *albu-minous* cells, fibres and *sclereids*).

Sieve Tubes

The sieve-tube cells lack a nucleus, have very few vacuoles, but contain other organelles such as ribosomes. The endo-plasmic reticulum is concentrated at the lateral walls. Sieve-tube members are joined end to end to form a tube that conducts food materials throughout the plant. The end walls of these cells have many small pores and are called sieve plates and have enlarged plasmodesmata.

Companion Cells

The survival of sieve-tube members depends on a close association with the *companion cells*. All of the cellular functions of a sieve-tube element are carried out by the (much smaller) companion cell, a typical plant cell, except the companion cell usually has a larger number of ribosomes and mitochondria. This is because the companion cell is more metabolically active than a 'typical' plant cell. The cytoplasm of a companion cell is connected to the sieve-tube element by plasmodesmata.

There are three types of companion cell.

1. **Ordinary companions cells** - which have smooth walls and few or no plasmodesmata connections to cells other than the sieve tube.
2. **Transfer cells** - which have much folded walls that are adjacent to non-sieve cells, allowing for larger areas of transfer. They are specialised in scavenging solutes from those in the cell walls which are actively pumped requiring energy.

3. **Intermediary cells** - which have smooth walls and numerous plasmodesmata connecting them to other cells.

The first two types of cell collect solutes through apoplastic (cell wall) transfers, whilst the third type can collect solutes symplastically through the plasmodesmata connections.

Function

Unlike xylem (which is composed primarily of dead cells), the phloem is composed of still-living cells that transport sap. The sap is a water-based solution, but rich in sugars made by the photosynthetic areas. These sugars are transported to non-photosynthetic parts of the plant, such as the roots, or into storage structures, such as tubers or bulbs.

The *Pressure flow hypothesis* was a hypothesis proposed by Ernst Munch in 1930 that explained the mechanism of phloem translocation A high concentration of organic substance inside cells of the phloem at a source, such as a leaf, creates a diffusion gradient that draws water into the cells. Movement occurs by bulk flow; phloem sap moves from *sugar source*s to *sugar sinks* by means of turgor pressure. A sugar source is any part of the plant that is producing or releasing sugar. During the plant's growth period, usually during the spring, storage organs such as the roots are sugar sources, and the plant's many growing areas are sugar sinks. The movement in phloem is bidirectional, whereas, in xylem cells, it is unidirectional (upward).

After the growth period, when the meristems are dormant, the leaves are sources, and storage organs are sinks. Developing seed-bearing organs (such as fruit) are always sinks. Because of this multi-directional flow, coupled with the fact that sap cannot move with ease between adjacent sieve-tubes, it is not unusual for sap in adjacent sieve-tubes to be flowing in opposite directions.

While movement of water and minerals through the xylem is driven by negative pressures (tension) most of the time, movement through the phloem is driven by positive hydrostatic pressures. This process is termed *translocation*, and is accomplished by a process called *phloem loading* and *unloading*. Cells in a sugar source "load" a sieve-tube element by actively transporting solute molecules into it. This causes water to move into the sieve-tube element by osmosis, creating pressure that pushes the sap down the tube. In sugar sinks, cells actively transport solutes *out* of the sieve-tube elements, producing the exactly opposite effect.

Some plants however appear not to load phloem by active transport. In these cases a mechanism known as the polymer trap mechanism was proposed by Robert Turgeon. In this case small sugars such as sucrose move into intermediary cells through narrow plasmodesmata, where they are polymerised to raffinose and other larger oligosaccharides. Now they are unable to move back, but can proceed through wider plasmodesmata into the sieve tube element.

The symplastic phloem loading is confined mostly to plants in tropical rain forests and is seen as more primitive. The actively-transported apoplastic phloem loading is viewed as more advanced, as it is found in the later-evolved plants, and particularly in those in temperate and arid conditions. This mechanism may therefore have allowed plants to colonise the cooler locations.

Organic molecules such as sugars, amino acids, certain hormones, and even messenger RNAs are transported in the phloem through sieve tube elements.

Girdling

Because phloem tubes sit on the outside of the xylem in most plants, a tree or other plant can be effectively killed by stripping away the bark in a ring on the trunk or stem. With the phloem destroyed, nutrients cannot reach the roots and the tree/plant will die. Trees located in areas with animals such as beavers are vulnerable since beavers chew off the bark at a fairly precise height. This process is known as girdling, and can be used for agricultural purposes. For example, enormous fruits and vegetables seen at fairs and carnivals are produced via girdling. A farmer would place a girdle at base of a large branch, and remove all but one fruit/vegetable from that branch. Thus, all the sugars manufactured by leaves on that branch have no sinks to go to but the one fruit/vegetable which thus expands to many times normal size.

Origin

The phloem originates, and grows outwards from, meristematic cells in the vascular cambium. Phloem is produced in phases. *Primary* phloem is laid down by the apical meristem. *Secondary* phloem is laid down by the vascular cambium to the inside of the established layer(s) of phloem.

WOOD

Wood is an organic material; in the strict sense it is produced as secondary xylem in the stems of trees (and other woody plants). In a living tree it conducts water and nutrients to the leaves and other growing tissues, and has a support function, enabling woody plants to reach large sizes or to stand up for themselves. However, wood may also refer to other plant materials with comparable properties, and to material engineered from wood, or wood chips or fiber.

People have used wood for millennia for many purposes, primarily as a fuel or as a construction material for making houses, tools, weapons, furniture, packaging, artworks, and paper. Wood can be dated by carbon dating and in some species by dendrochronology to make inferences about when a wooden object was created. The year-to-year variation in tree-ring widths and isotopic abundances gives clues to the prevailing climate at that time.

Formation

Wood, in the strict sense, is yielded by trees, which increase in diameter by the formation, between the existing wood and the inner bark, of new woody layers which envelop the entire stem, living branches, and roots. Technically this is known as secondary growth; it is the result of cell division in the vascular cambium, a lateral meristem, and subsequent expansion of the new cells.

Growth Rings

Where there are clear seasons, growth can occur in a discrete annual or seasonal pattern, leading to growth rings; these can usually be most clearly seen on the end of a log, but are also visible on the other surfaces. If these seasons are annual these growth rings are referred to as annual rings. Where there is no seasonal difference growth rings are likely to be indistinct or absent.

If there are differences within a growth ring then the part of a growth ring nearest the center of the tree, and formed early in the growing season when growth is rapid, is usually composed of wider elements. It is usually lighter in color than that near the outer portion of the ring, and is known as earlywood or springwood. The outer portion formed later in the season is then known as the latewood or summerwood. However, there are major differences, depending on the kind of wood.

Knots

A knot is a particular type of imperfection in a piece of wood; it will affect the technical properties of the wood, usually for the worse, but may be exploited for artistic effect. In a longitudinally-sawn plank, a knot will appear as a roughly circular "solid" (usually darker) piece of wood around which the grain of the rest of the wood "flows" (parts and rejoins). Within a knot, the direction of the wood (grain direction) is up to 90 degrees different from the grain direction of the regular wood.

In the tree a knot is either the base of a side branch or a dormant bud. A knot (when the base of a side branch) is conical in shape (hence the roughly circular cross-section) with the tip at the point in stem diameter at which the plant's cambium was located when the branch formed as a bud.

During the development of a tree, the lower limbs often die, but may persist for a time, sometimes years. Subsequent layers of growth of the attaching stem are no longer intimately joined with the dead limb, but are grown around it. Hence, dead branches produce knots which are not attached, and likely to drop out after the tree has been sawn into boards.

In grading lumber and structural timber, knots are classified according to their form, size, soundness, and the firmness with which they are held in place. This firmness is affected by, among other factors, the length of time for which the branch was dead while the attaching stem continued to grow.

Knots materially affect cracking (known in the industry as checking) and warping, ease in working, and cleavability of timber. They are defects which weaken timber and lower its value for structural purposes where strength is an important consideration. The weakening effect is much more serious when timber is subjected to forces perpendicular to the grain and/or tension than where under load along the grain and/or compression. The extent to which knots affect the strength of a beam depends upon their position, size, number, and condition. A knot on the upper side is compressed, while one on the lower side is subjected to tension. If there is a season check in the knot, as is often the case, it will offer little resistance to this tensile stress. Small knots, however, may be located along the neutral plane of a beam and increase the strength by preventing longitudinal shearing. Knots in a board or plank are least injurious when they extend through it at right angles to its broadest surface. Knots which occur near the ends of a beam do not weaken it. Sound knots which occur in the central portion one-fourth the height of the beam from either edge are not serious defects.

Knots do not necessarily influence the stiffness of structural timber, this will depend on the size and location. Stiffness and elastic strength are more dependent upon the sound wood than upon localized defects. The breaking strength is very susceptible to defects. Sound knots do not weaken wood when subject to compression parallel to the grain.

In some decorative applications, to add visual interest, wood with knots may be preferred. The traditional style of playing the Basque xylophon *txalaparta* involves hitting the right knots to obtain different tones.

Heartwood and Sapwood

Heartwood is wood that has become more resistant to decay as a result of deposition of chemical substances (a genetically programmed process). Once heartwood formation is complete, the heartwood is dead. It appears in a cross-section as a usually colored circle, usually following the growth rings in shape. Heartwood may be much darker than living wood. However, other processes, such as decay, can discolor wood, even in woody plants that do not form heartwood, with a similar color difference, leading to confusion. Some uncertainty still exists as to whether heartwood is truly dead, as it can still chemically react to decay organisms, but only once.

Sapwood is the younger, outermost wood; in the growing tree it is living wood, and its principal functions are to conduct water from the roots to the leaves and to store up and give back according to the season the reserves prepared in the leaves. However, by the time they become competent to conduct water, all xylem tracheids and vessels have lost their cytoplasm and the cells are therefore functionally dead. All wood in a tree is first formed as sapwood. The more leaves a tree bears and the more vigorous its growth, the larger the volume of sapwood required. Hence trees making rapid growth in the open have thicker sapwood for their size than trees of the same species growing in dense forests. Sometimes trees (of species that do form heartwood) grown in the open may become of considerable size, 30 cm or more in diameter, before any heartwood begins to form, for example, in second-growth hickory, or open-grown pines.

The term *heartwood* derives solely from its position and not from any vital importance to the tree. This is evidenced by the fact that a tree can thrive with its heart completely decayed. Some species begin to form heartwood very early in life, so having only a thin layer of live sapwood, while in others the change comes slowly. Thin sapwood is characteristic of such species as chestnut, black locust, mulberry, osage-orange, and sassafras, while in maple, ash, hickory, hackberry, beech, and pine, thick sapwood is the rule. Others never form heartwood.

There is no definite relation between the annual rings of growth and the amount of sapwood. Within the same species the cross-sectional area of the sapwood is very roughly proportional to the size of the crown of the tree. If the rings are narrow, more of them are required than where they are wide. As the tree gets larger, the sapwood must necessarily become thinner or increase materially in volume. Sapwood is thicker in the upper portion of the trunk of a tree than near the base, because the age and the diameter of the upper sections are less.

When a tree is very young it is covered with limbs almost, if not entirely, to the ground, but as it grows older some or all of them will eventually die and are either broken off or fall off. Subsequent growth of wood may completely conceal the stubs which will however remain as knots. No matter how smooth and clear a log is on the outside, it is more or less knotty near the middle. Consequently, the sapwood of an old tree, and particularly of a forest-grown tree, will be freer from knots than the inner heartwood. Since in most uses of wood, knots are defects that weaken the timber and interfere with its ease of working and other properties, it follows that a given piece of sapwood, because of its position in the tree, may well be stronger than a piece of heartwood from the same tree.

It is remarkable that the inner heartwood of old trees remains as sound as it usually does, since in many cases it is hundreds of years, and in a few instances thousands of years, old. Every broken limb or root, or deep wound from fire, insects, or falling timber, may afford an entrance for decay, which, once started, may penetrate to all parts of the trunk. The larvae of many insects bore into the trees and their tunnels remain indefinitely as sources of weakness. Whatever advantages, however, that sapwood may have in this connection are due solely to its relative age and position.

If a tree grows all its life in the open and the conditions of soil and site remain unchanged, it will make its most rapid growth in youth, and gradually decline. The annual rings of growth are for many years quite wide, but later they become narrower and narrower. Since each succeeding ring is laid down on the outside of the wood previously formed, it follows that unless a tree materially increases its production of wood from year to year, the rings must necessarily become thinner as the trunk gets wider. As a tree reaches maturity its crown becomes more open and the annual wood production is lessened, thereby reducing still more the width of the growth rings. In the case of forest-grown trees so much depends upon the competition of the trees in their struggle for light and nourishment that periods of rapid and slow growth may alternate. Some trees, such as southern oaks, maintain the same width of ring for hundreds of years. Upon the whole, however, as a tree gets larger in diameter the width of the growth rings decreases.

Different pieces of wood cut from a large tree may differ decidedly, particularly if the tree is big and mature. In some trees, the wood laid on late in the life of a tree is softer, lighter, weaker, and more even-textured than that produced earlier, but in other trees, the reverse applies. This may or may not correspond to heartwood and sapwood. In a large log the sapwood, because of the time in the life of the tree when it was grown, may be inferior in hardness, strength, and toughness to equally sound heartwood from the same log. In a smaller tree, the reverse may be true.

Different Woods

There is a strong relationship between the properties of wood and the properties of the particular tree that yielded it. For every tree species there is a range of density for the wood it yields. There is a rough correlation between density of a wood and its strength (mechanical properties). For example, while mahogany is a medium-dense hardwood which is excellent for fine furniture crafting, balsa is light, making it useful for model building. The densest wood may be black ironwood.

It is common to classify wood as either softwood or hardwood. The wood from conifers (e.g. pine) is called softwood, and the wood from dicotyledons (usually broad-leaved trees, e.g. oak) is called hardwood. These names are a bit misleading, as hardwoods are not necessarily hard, and softwoods are not necessarily soft. The well-known balsa (a hardwood) is actually softer than any commercial softwood. Conversely, some softwoods (e.g. yew) are harder than most hardwoods.

Colour

In species which show a distinct difference between heartwood and sapwood the natural colour of heartwood is usually darker than that of the sapwood, and very frequently the contrast is conspicuous. This is produced by deposits in the heartwood of chemical substances, so that a dramatic color difference does not mean a dramatic difference in the mechanical properties of heartwood and sapwood, although there may be a dramatic chemical difference.

Some experiments on very resinous Longleaf Pine specimens indicate an increase in strength, due to the resin which increases the strength when dry. Such resin-saturated heartwood is called "fat lighter". Structures built of fat lighter are almost impervious to rot and termites; however they are very flammable. Stumps of old longleaf pines are often dug, split into small pieces and sold as kindling for fires. Stumps thus dug may actually remain a century or more since being cut. Spruce impregnated with crude resin and dried is also greatly increased in strength thereby.

Since the latewood of a growth ring is usually darker in colour than the earlywood, this fact may be used in judging the density, and therefore the hardness and strength of the material. This is particularly the case with coniferous woods. In ring-porous woods the vessels of the early wood not infrequently appear on a finished surface as darker than the denser latewood, though on cross sections of heartwood the reverse is commonly true. Except in the manner just stated the colour of wood is no indication of strength.

Abnormal discolouration of wood often denotes a diseased condition, indicating unsoundness. The black check in western hemlock is the result of insect attacks. The reddish-brown streaks so common in hickory and certain other woods are mostly the result of injury by birds. The discolouration is merely an indication of an injury, and in all probability does not of itself affect the properties of the wood. Certain rot-producing fungi impart to wood characteristic colours which thus become symptomatic of weakness; however an attractive effect known as spalting produced by this process is often considered a desirable characteristic. Ordinary sap-staining is due to fungous growth, but does not necessarily produce a weakening effect.

Structure

Wood is a heterogeneous, hygroscopic, cellular and anisotropic material. It is composed of cells, and the cell walls are composed of microfibrils of cellulose (40%-50%) and hemicellulose (15%-25%) impregnated with lignin (15%-30%).

In coniferous or softwood species the wood cells are mostly of one kind, tracheids, and as a result the material is much more uniform in structure than that of most hardwoods. There are no vessels ("pores") in coniferous wood such as one sees so prominently in oak and ash, for example.

The structure of hardwoods is more complex The water conducting capability is mostly taken care of by vessels: in some cases (oak, chestnut, ash) these are quite large and distinct, in others (buckeye, poplar, willow) too small to be seen without a hand lens. In discussing such woods it is customary to divide them into two large classes, *ring-porous* and *diffuse-porous*. In ring-porous species, such as ash, black locust, catalpa, chestnut, elm, hickory, mulberry, and oak, the larger vessels or pores (as cross sections of vessels are called) are localized in the part of the growth ring formed in spring, thus forming a region of more or less open and porous tissue. The rest of the ring, produced in summer, is made up of smaller vessels and a much greater proportion of wood fibres. These fibres are the elements which give strength and toughness to wood, while the vessels are a source of weakness.

In diffuse-porous woods the pores are evenly-sized so that the water conducting capability is scattered throughout the growth ring instead of being collected in a band or row. Examples of this kind of wood are basswood, birch, buckeye, maple, poplar, and willow. Some species, such as walnut and cherry, are on the border between the two classes, forming an intermediate group.

Earlywood and Latewood in Softwood

In temperate softwoods there often is a marked difference between latewood and earlywood. The latewood will be denser than that formed early in the season. When examined under a microscope the cells of dense latewood are seen to be very thick-walled and with very small cell cavities, while those formed first in the season have thin walls and large cell cavities. The strength is in the walls, not the cavities. Hence the greater the proportion of latewood the greater the density and strength. In choosing a piece of pine where strength or stiffness is the important consideration, the principal thing to observe is the comparative amounts of earlywood and latewood. The width of ring is not nearly so important as the proportion and nature of the latewood in the ring.

If a heavy piece of pine is compared with a lightweight piece it will be seen at once that the heavier one contains a larger proportion of latewood than the other, and is therefore showing more clearly demarcated growth rings. In white pines there is not much contrast between the different parts of the ring, and as a result the wood is very uniform in texture and is easy to work. In hard pines, on the other hand, the latewood is very dense and is deep-colored, presenting a very decided contrast to the soft, straw-colored earlywood.

It is not only the proportion of latewood, but also its quality, that counts. In specimens that show a very large proportion of latewood it may be noticeably more porous and weigh considerably less than the latewood in pieces that contain but little. One can judge comparative density, and therefore to some extent strength, by visual inspection.

No satisfactory explanation can as yet be given for the exact mechanisms determining the formation of earlywood and latewood. Several factors may be involved. In conifers, at least, rate of growth alone does not determine the proportion of the two portions of the ring, for in some cases the wood of slow growth is very hard and heavy, while in others the opposite is true. The quality of the site where the tree grows undoubtedly affects the character of the wood formed, though it is not possible to formulate a rule governing it. In general, however, it may be said that where strength or ease of working is essential, woods of moderate to slow growth should be chosen.

Earlywood and Latewood in Ring-porous Woods

In ring-porous woods each season's growth is always well defined, because the large pores formed early in the season abut on the denser tissue of the year before.

In the case of the ring-porous hardwoods there seems to exist a pretty definite relation between the rate of growth of timber and its properties. This may be briefly summed up in the general statement that the more rapid the growth or the wider the rings of growth, the heavier, harder, stronger, and stiffer the wood. This, it must be remembered, applies only to ring-porous woods such as oak, ash, hickory, and others of the same group, and is, of course, subject to some exceptions and limitations.

In ring-porous woods of good growth it is usually the latewood in which the thick-walled, strength-giving fibers are most abundant. As the breadth of ring diminishes, this latewood is reduced so that very slow growth produces comparatively light, porous wood composed of thin-walled vessels and wood parenchyma. In good oak these large vessels of the earlywood occupy from 6 to 10 per cent of the volume of the log, while in inferior material they may make up 25 per cent or more. The latewood of good oak is dark colored and firm, and consists mostly of thick-walled fibers which form one-half or more of the wood. In inferior oak, this latewood is much reduced both in quantity and quality. Such variation is very largely the result of rate of growth.

Wide-ringed wood is often called "second-growth", because the growth of the young timber in open stands after the old trees have been removed is more rapid than in trees in a closed forest, and in the manufacture of articles where strength is an important consideration such "second-growth" hardwood material is preferred. This is particularly the case in the choice of hickory for handles and spokes. Here not only strength, but toughness and resilience are important. The results of a series of tests on hickory by the U.S. Forest Service show that:

> "The work or shock-resisting ability is greatest in wide-ringed wood that has from 5 to 14 rings per inch (rings 1.8-5 mm thick), is fairly constant from 14 to 38 rings per inch (rings 0.7-1.8 mm thick), and decreases rapidly from 38 to 47 rings per inch (rings 0.5-0.7 mm thick). The strength at maximum load is not so great with the most rapid-growing wood; it is maximum with from 14 to 20 rings per inch (rings 1.3-1.8 mm thick), and again becomes less as the wood becomes more closely ringed. The natural deduction is that wood of first-class mechanical value shows from 5 to 20 rings per inch (rings 1.3-5 mm thick) and that slower growth yields poorer stock. Thus the inspector or buyer of hickory should discriminate against timber that has

more than 20 rings per inch (rings less than 1.3 mm thick). Exceptions exist, however, in the case of normal growth upon dry situations, in which the slow-growing material may be strong and tough."

The effect of rate of growth on the qualities of chestnut wood is summarized by the same authority as follows:

"When the rings are wide, the transition from spring wood to summer wood is gradual, while in the narrow rings the spring wood passes into summer wood abruptly. The width of the spring wood changes but little with the width of the annual ring, so that the narrowing or broadening of the annual ring is always at the expense of the summer wood. The narrow vessels of the summer wood make it richer in wood substance than the spring wood composed of wide vessels. Therefore, rapid-growing specimens with wide rings have more wood substance than slow-growing trees with narrow rings. Since the more the wood substance the greater the weight, and the greater the weight the stronger the wood, chestnuts with wide rings must have stronger wood than chestnuts with narrow rings. This agrees with the accepted view that sprouts (which always have wide rings) yield better and stronger wood than seedling chestnuts, which grow more slowly in diameter."

Earlywood and Latewood in Diffuse-porous Woods

In the diffuse-porous woods, the demarcation between rings is not always so clear and in some cases is almost (if not entirely) invisible to the unaided eye. Conversely, when there is a clear demarcation there may not be a noticeable difference in structure within the growth ring.

In diffuse-porous woods, as has been stated, the vessels or pores are even-sized, so that the water conducting capability is scattered throughout the ring instead of collected in the earlywood. The effect of rate of growth is, therefore, not the same as in the ring-porous woods, approaching more nearly the conditions in the conifers. In general it may be stated that such woods of medium growth afford stronger material than when very rapidly or very slowly grown. In many uses of wood, total strength is not the main consideration. If ease of working is prized, wood should be chosen with regard to its uniformity of texture and straightness of grain, which will in most cases occur when there is little contrast between the latewood of one season's growth and the earlywood of the next.

Monocot Wood

Structural material that roughly (in its gross handling characteristics) resembles ordinary, 'dicot' or conifer wood is produced by a number of monocot plants, and these are also usually called wood. Of these, bamboo, botanically a member of the grass family, has considerable economic importance, larger culms being widely used as a building and construction material in their own right and, these days, in the manufacture of engineered flooring, panels and veneer. Another major plant group that produce material that often is called wood are the palms. Of much less importance are plants such as *Pandanus*, *Dracaena* and *Cordyline*. With all this material, the structure and composition of the structural material is quite different from ordinary wood.

Water Content

Water occurs in living wood in three conditions, namely:

1. in the cell walls;
2. in the protoplasmic contents of the cells; and
3. as free water in the cell cavities and spaces.

In heartwood it occurs only in the first and last forms. Wood that is thoroughly air-dried retains from 8-16% of water in the cell walls, and none, or practically none, in the other forms. Even oven-dried wood retains a small percentage of moisture, but for all except chemical purposes, may be considered absolutely dry.

The general effect of the water content upon the wood substance is to render it softer and more pliable. A similar effect of common observation is in the softening action of water on paper or cloth. Within certain limits, the greater the water content, the greater its softening effect.

Drying produces a decided increase in the strength of wood, particularly in small specimens. An extreme example is the case of a completely dry spruce block 5 cm in section, which will sustain a permanent load four times as great as that which a green (undried) block of the same size will support.

The greatest increase due to drying is in the ultimate crushing strength, and strength at elastic limit in endwise compression; these are followed by the modulus of rupture, and stress at elastic limit in cross-bending, while the modulus of elasticity is least affected.

Root

In vascular plants, the root is the organ of a plant that typically lies below the surface of the soil. This is not always the case, however, since a root can also be aerial (growing above the ground) or aerating (growing up above the ground or especially above water). Furthermore, a stem normally occurring below ground is not exceptional either. So, it is better to define root as a part of a plant body that bears no leaves, and therefore also lacks nodes. There are also important internal structural differences between stems and roots. The two major functions of roots are:

1. absorption of water and inorganic nutrients; and
2. anchoring of the plant body to the ground.

In response to the concentration of nutrients, roots also synthesise cytokinin, which acts as a signal as to how fast the shoots can grow. Roots often function in storage of food and nutrients. The roots of most vascular plant species enter into symbiosis with certain fungi to form mycorrhizas, and a large range of other organisms including bacteria also closely associate with roots.

Root Growth

Early root growth is one of the functions of the apical meristem located near the tip of the root. The meristem cells more or less continuously divide, producing more meristem, root cap cells (these are sacrificed to protect the meristem), and undifferentiated root cells. The latter become the primary tissues of the root, first undergoing elongation, a process that pushes the root tip forward in the growing medium. Gradually these cells differentiate and mature into specialized cells of the root tissues.

Roots will generally grow in any direction where the correct environment of air, mineral nutrients and water exists to meet the plant's needs. Roots will not grow in dry soil. Over time, given the right conditions, roots can crack foundations, snap water lines, and lift sidewalks. At germination, roots grow downward due to gravitropism, the growth mechanism of plants that also causes the shoot to grow upward. In some plants (such as ivy), the "root" actually clings to walls and structures.

Growth from apical meristems is known as primary growth, which encompasses all elongation. Secondary growth encompasses all growth in diameter, a major component of woody plant tissues and many nonwoody plants. For example, storage roots of sweet potato have secondary growth but are not woody. Secondary growth occurs at the lateral meristems, namely the vascular cambium and cork cambium. The former forms secondary xylem and secondary phloem, while the latter forms the periderm.

In plants with secondary growth, the vascular cambium, originating between the xylem and the phloem, forms a cylinder of tissue along the stem and root. The cambium layer forms new cells on both the inside and outside of the cambium cylinder, with those on the inside forming secondary xylem cells, and those on the outside forming secondary phloem cells. As secondary xylem accumulates, the "girth" (lateral dimensions) of the stem and root increases. As a result, tissues beyond the secondary phloem (including the epidermis and cortex, in many cases) tend to be pushed outward and are eventually "sloughed off" (shed).

At this point, the cork cambium begins to form the periderm, consisting of protective cork cells containing suberin. In roots, the cork cambium originates in the pericycle, a component of the vascular cylinder.

The vascular cambium produces new layers of secondary xylem annually. The xylem vessels are dead at maturity but are responsible for most water transport through the vascular tissue in stems and roots.

Types of Roots

A true root system consists of a primary root and secondary roots (or lateral roots).

The primary root originates in the radicle of the seedling. It is the first part of the root to be originated. During its growth it rebranches to form the lateral roots. It usually grows downwards. Generally, two categories are recognized:

1. **the taproot system:** the primary root is prominent and has a single, dominant axis; there are fibrous secondary roots running outward. Usually allows for deeper roots capable of reaching low water tables. Most common in dicots. The main function of the taproot is to store food.
2. **the diffuse root system:** the primary root is not dominant; the whole root system is fibrous and branches in all directions. Most common in monocots. The main function of the fibrous root is to anchor the plant.

Specialized Roots

The roots, or parts of roots, of many plant species have become specialized to serve adaptive purposes besides the two primary functions described in the introduction.

- **Adventitious roots** arise out-of-sequence from the more usual root formation of branches of a primary root, and instead originate from the stem, branches, leaves, or old woody roots. They commonly occur in monocots and pteridophytes, but also in many dicots, such as clover (*Trifolium*), ivy (*Hedera*), strawberry (*Fragaria*) and willow (*Salix*). Most aerial roots and stilt roots are adventitious. In some conifers adventitious roots can form the largest part of the root system.
- **Aerating roots (or pneumatophores):** roots rising above the ground, especially above water such as in some mangrove genera (*Avicennia, Sonneratia*). In some plants like *Avicennia* the erect roots have a large number of breathing pores for exchange of gases.
- **Aerial roots**: roots entirely above the ground, such as in ivy (*Hedera*) or in epiphytic orchids. They function as prop roots, as in maize or anchor roots or as the trunk in strangler fig.
- **Contractile roots**: they pull bulbs or corms of monocots, such as hyacinth and lily, and some taproots, such as dandelion, deeper in the soil through expanding radially and contracting longitudinally. They have a wrinkled surface.
- **Coarse roots**: Roots that have undergone secondary thickening and have a woody structure. These roots have some ability to absorb water and nutrients, but their main function is transport and to provide a structure to connect the smaller diameter, fine roots to the rest of the plant.

- **Fine roots**: Primary roots usually <2 mm diameter that have the function of water and nutrient uptake. They are often heavily branched and support mycorrhizas. These roots may be short lived, but are replaced by the plant in an ongoing process of root 'turnover'.
- **Haustorial roots**: roots of parasitic plants that can absorb water and nutrients from another plant, such as in mistletoe (*Viscum album*) and dodder.
- **Propagative roots**: roots that form adventitious buds that develop into above ground shoots, termed suckers, which form new plants, as in Canada thistle, cherry and many others.
- **Proteoid roots** or cluster roots: dense clusters of rootlets of limited growth that develop under low phosphate or low iron conditions in Proteaceae and some plants from the following families Betulaceae, Casuarinaceae, Eleagnaceae, Moraceae, Fabaceae and Myricaceae.
- **Stilt roots**: these are adventitious support roots, common among mangroves. They grow down from lateral branches, branching in the soil.
- **Storage roots**: these roots are modified for storage of food or water, such as carrots and beets. They include some taproots and tuberous roots.
- **Structural roots**: large roots that have undergone considerable secondary thickening and provide mechanical support to woody plants and trees.
- **Surface roots**: These proliferate close below the soil surface, exploiting water and easily available nutrients. Where conditions are close to optimum in the surface layers of soil, the growth of surface roots is encouraged and they commonly become the dominant roots.
- **Tuberous roots**: A portion of a root swells for food or water storage, e.g. sweet potato. A type of storage root distinct from taproot.

Rooting Depths

The distribution of vascular plant roots within soil depends on plant form, the spatial and temporal availability of water and nutrients, and the physical properties of the soil. The deepest roots are generally found in deserts and temperate coniferous forests; the shallowest in tundra, boreal forest and temperate grasslands. The deepest observed living root, at least 60 m below the ground surface, was observed during the excavation of an open-pit mine in Arizona, U.S.A. Some roots can grow as deep as the tree is high. The majority of roots on most plants are however found relatively close to the surface where nutrient availability and aeration are more favourable for growth. Rooting depth may be physically restricted by rock or compacted soil close below the surface, or by anaerobic soil conditions.

Root Architecture

The pattern of development of a root system is termed 'root architecture', and is important in providing a plant with a secure supply of nutrients and water as well as anchorage and support. The architecture of a root system can be considered in a similar way to above-ground architecture of a plant - i.e. in terms of the size, branching and distribution of the component parts. In roots, the architecture of fine roots and coarse roots can both be described by variation in topology and distribution of biomass within and between roots. Having a balanced architecture allows fine roots to exploit soil efficiently around a plant, but the 'plastic' nature of root growth allows the plant to then concentrate its resources where nutrients and water are more easily available. A balanced coarse root architecture, with roots distributed relatively evenly around the stem base, is necessary to provide support to larger plants and trees.

Evolutionary History

The fossil record of roots - or rather, infilled voids where roots rotted after death - spans back to the late Silurian, but their identification is difficult, because casts and molds of roots are so similar in appearance to animal burrows - although they can be discriminated on the basis of a range of features.

Economic Importance

The term root crops refers to any edible underground plant structure, but many root crops are actually stems, such as potato tubers. Edible roots include cassava, sweet potato, beet, carrot, rutabaga, turnip, parsnip, radish, yam and horseradish. Spices obtained from roots include sassafras, angelica, sarsaparilla and licorice.

Sugar beet is an important source of sugar. Yam roots are a source of estrogen compounds used in birth control pills. The fish poison and insecticide rotenone is obtained from roots of *Lonchocarpus* spp. Important medicines from roots are ginseng, aconite, ipecac, gentian and reserpine. Several legumes that have nitrogen-fixing root nodules are used as green manure crops, which provide nitrogen fertilizer for other crops when plowed under. Specialized bald cypress roots, termed knees, are sold as souvenirs, lamp bases and carved into folk art. Native Americans used the flexible roots of white spruce for basketry.

Tree roots can heave and destroy concrete sidewalks and crush or clog buried pipes. The aerial roots of strangler fig have damaged ancient Mayan temples in Central America and the temple of Angkor Wat in Cambodia.

Vegetative propagation of plants via cuttings depends on adventitious root formation. Hundreds of millions of plants are propagated via cuttings annually including chrysanthemum, poinsettia, carnation, ornamental shrubs and many houseplants.

Roots can also protect the environment by holding the soil to prevent soil erosion.

PLANT CUTTING

Plant cutting, also known as striking/cloning, is a technique for vegetatively (a sexually) propagating plants in which a piece of the source plant containing at least one stem cell is placed in a suitable medium such as moist soil, potting mix, coir or rock wool. The cutting produces new roots, stems, or both, and thus becomes a new plant independent of the parent.

Technique

Typically, striking is a simple process in which a small amount of the parent plant is removed. This removed piece, called the *cutting*, is then encouraged to grow as an independent plant.

However, to have a fair degree of success, the practice of taking cuttings is not as straightforward. Since the cutting has no root system of its own, it is likely to die from dehydration if the proper conditions are not met.

Thus, to have a fair amount of cuttings catching on, the cutting should have:

- a moist medium. The medium cannot, however, be too wet lest the cutting rot. A number of media are used in this process, including but not limited to soil, perlite, vermiculite, coir, rock wool, expanded clay, and even water given the right conditions.
- a humid environment (this generally means placing the cuttings under a plastic sheet or in another confined space where the air can be kept moist).
- partial shade (to prevent the cutting from drying out).

After cuttings are placed in the medium, they are watered thoroughly with a fine mist. The fine mist of a nozzle sprayer or a spray mist bottle are often used. After the initial watering, the medium is allowed to almost dry out before misting again, with the aim to keep the soil moist but not wet and waterlogged. A fine mist is used to avoid disturbing plants.

In addition, the cutting needs to be taken correctly; this means:

- at the right time; in temperate countries, stem cuttings of young wood need to be taken in spring, of hardened wood they need to be taken in winter.
- with the right size and amount of foliage; length of stem cuttings of soft wood for example need to be between 5-15cm and of hard wood between 20-25cm. Also, the foliage of soft wood stem cuttings needs to be removed by 2/3 and of hard wood stem cuttings, complete foliage removal is necessary.

Also, though not essential, several compounds may be used to promote the formation of roots such as the auxins. Among the commonly used ones is indole-3-butyric acid, or IBA, used as a powder, liquid solution or gel. This compound is applied either to the cut tip of the cutting or as a foliar spray.

Types of Cuttings

Many vegetative parts of a plant can be used. The most common methods are:

- Stem cuttings, in which a piece of stem is part buried in the soil, including at least one leaf node. It produces new roots, usually at the node.
- Root cuttings, in which a section of root is buried just below the soil surface, and produces new shoots.
- Scion cuttings; which are dormant 'ligneous' woody twigs.

- Eye cuttings, which are pieces of foliated or defoliated stalks with one or more eyes.
- Leaf cuttings, in which a leaf is placed on moist soil. These have to develop both new stems and new roots. Some leaves will produce one plant at the base of the leaf. In some species, multiple new plants can be produced at many places on one leaf, and these can be induced by cutting the leaf veins.

Although some species, such as willow, blackberry and pelargoniums can be struck simply by sticking into moist ground, most species require more attention. Most species, require humid, warm, partially shaded conditions to strike, thus requiring the approach above to be followed. Particularly difficult species may need cool air above and warm soil. In addition, with many more difficult strikings, one would also prefer to use the type of cutting that has the most chance of success with that particular plant species.

Providing the Right Soil

Depending on the type of soil with which you start, several additives may need adding to create good soil for cuttings. These additions may include:

- chalk; to increase the pH-value of the soil; a Ph of 6-6, 5 is to be maintained.
- organic substance/humus; to increase nutrient load; keep to a bare minimum though.
- sand/gravel; to increase the soil's water permeability.

For example with plain potting soil, you would want to add 1/3 sand to make suitable soil for cuttings.

Providing the Right Humidity

Although several options can be used here, usually semi-white plastic is used to cover the cuttings. The soil below and from the cuttings themselves is kept moist. Aerate once in a while to prevent formation of molds.

Rooting Substance

Rooting hormone may be used to facilitate striking, yet is generally not the most important factor in the process. However it is helpful with especially hard plant species.

Many root promoting products from various companies are offered on the market. Substances with rooting effects are almost inevitably based on signaling activity of plant hormone auxin and various auxin compounds (IAA, NAA, IBA,) were implemented in various commercially available products. If you do not want to buy similar product on market, you may try prepare some rooting substance in more traditional way.

Homemade Rooting Supplements

When starting a new plant from a leaf or stem cutting, the cutting will be more likely to form roots and create a new plant if a rooting hormone is used.

While commercial rooting hormone can be used there are organic homemade versions that work as well.

To make rooting hormone, soak the yellow-tipped shoots of a weeping willow tree in water. A tea made from the bark of a willow tree is also effective. When using the shoots or bark, soak them for 24 hours prior to using.

Some people have found that honey, though not containing hormones, makes an effective rooting substance as well.

Using Rooting Hormone or Supplement

Leaf cuttings: Certain plants, such as African Violet, Geranium, Begonia and others, can be propagated with leaf cuttings. Using a sharp knife, cut off a healthy leaf at the point where it joins the stem. Insert the cut part, called a petiole, into the rooting hormone. Place the end into a small container of light potting soil in which you make a small hole with a pencil.

Making a hole prior to planting assures that the rooting hormone or other substance will not be brushed off the cutting when you plant it. Perlite, Vermiculite, and/or water-soaked Sphagnum moss can be added to potting soil to make the soil light. Make sure the leaf is leaning slightly so that the new plants will have plenty of light and not be shaded by the leaf.

Stem cuttings: These are treated just like leaf cuttings except you cut off a stem with several leaves instead of just one leaf. Remove the bottom leaves, leaving a few at the top. Proceed as with the leaf cutting.

In both instances, cover the pot with a plastic bag or inverted glass jar. This will keep moisture from evaporating and keep the cutting from wilting. Keep in a warm location with diffused light but out of direct sunlight. When there is indications of growth after about 3 to 6 weeks, transplant the new emerging plant into a new pot of potting soil. Continue to keep a humid environment for about 2 more weeks until active growth begins.

Stem Cuttings

In temperate countries, stem cuttings may be taken of soft (green or semi-ripe) wood and hard wood which has specific differences in practice. Stem cuttings of soft wood is taken in spring, while from hard wood, they are taken in winter. Also, of soft wood the upper branches are taken (with a length of 5-15cm) and with hard wood, the lower branches are taken instead (with a length of 20-25cm). Finally, soft wood cuttings are planted above ground and hard wood cuttings are totally submerged with soil. With hard wood cuttings, several cuttings are also bound together (to a bushel).

Grafting

History

Grafting with detached scions has been practiced for thousands of years. It was in use by the Chinese before

2000 B.C. and by the first known citizens of Mesopotamia. The practice was almost commonplace in ancient Greece.

Grafting is a method of asexual plant propagation widely used in agriculture and horticulture where the tissues of one plant are encouraged to fuse with those of another. It is most commonly used for the propagation of trees and shrubs grown commercially.

In most cases, one plant is selected for its roots, and this is called the stock or rootstock. The other plant is selected for its stems, leaves, flowers, or fruits and is called the scion. The scion contains the desired genes to be duplicated in future production by the stock/scion plant.

In stem grafting, a common grafting method, a shoot of a selected, desired plant cultivar is grafted onto the stock of another type. In another common form called budding, a dormant side bud is grafted on the stem of another stock plant, and when it has fused successfully, it is encouraged to grow by cutting out the stem above the new bud.

For successful grafting to take place, the vascular cambium tissues of the stock and scion plants must be placed in contact with each other. Both tissues must be kept alive until the graft has taken, usually a period of a few weeks. Successful grafting only requires that a vascular connection takes place between the two tissues. A physical weak point often still occurs at the graft, because the structural tissue of the two distinct plants, such as wood may not fuse.

Advantages for Grafting

- **Dwarfing**: To induce dwarfing or cold tolerance or other characteristics to the scion. Most apple trees in modern orchards are grafted dwarf or semi-dwarf trees planted at high density. They provide more fruit per unit of land, higher quality fruit, and reduce the danger of accidents by harvest crews working on ladders.

- **Ease of propagation**: Because the scion is difficult to propagate vegetatively by other means, such as by cuttings. In this case, cuttings of an easily rooted plant are used to provide a rootstock. In some cases, the scion may be easily propagated, but grafting may still be used because it is commercially the most cost-effective way of raising a particular type of plant.
- **Hybrid breeding**: To speed maturity of hybrids in fruit tree breeding programs. Hybrid seedlings may take ten or more years to flower and fruit on their own roots. Grafting can reduce the time to flowering and shorten the breeding program.
- **Hardiness**: Because the scion has weak roots or the roots of the stock plants have roots tolerant of difficult conditions. e.g. many showy Western Australian plants are sensitive to dieback on heavy soils, common in urban gardens, and are grafted onto hardier eastern Australian relatives. Grevilleas and eucalypts are examples.
- **Sturdiness** In order to provide a strong, tall trunk for certain ornamental shrubs and trees. In these cases, a graft is made at a desired height on a stock plant with a strong stem. This is used to raise 'standard' roses, which are rose bushes on a high stem, and it is also used for some ornamental trees, such as certain weeping cherries.
- **Pollen source**: To provide pollenizers. For example, in tightly planted or badly planned apple orchards of a single variety, limbs of crab apple may be grafted at regularly spaced intervals onto trees down rows, say every fourth tree. This takes care of pollen needs at blossom time, yet does not confuse pickers who might otherwise mix varieties while harvesting, as the mature crab apples are so distinct from other apple varieties.

- **Repair**: To repair damage to the trunk of a tree which would prohibit nutrient flow, such as the stripping of the bark by rodents which completely girdles the trunk. In this case a bridge graft may be used to connect the tissues receiving flow from the roots to the tissues above the damage which have been severed from the flow. Where a waterspout, sucker or sapling of the same species is growing nearby, any of these can be grafted to the area above the damage by a method called inarch grafting. These alternatives to scions must be of the correct length to span the gap of the wound.
- **Changing cultivars**: To change the cultivar in a fruit orchard to a more profitable cultivar, called *topworking*. It may be faster to graft a new cultivar onto existing limbs of established trees than to replant an entire orchard.
- **Maintain Consistency**: Apples are notorious for their genetic variability, even differing in multiple characteristics, such as, size, color, and flavor, of fruits located on the same tree. In the commercial farming industry, consistency is maintained by grafting a scion with desired fruit traits onto a hardy stock.

  An example of approach grafting by Axel Erlandson.
- **Curiosities.**
  - A practice sometimes carried out by gardeners is to graft related potatoes and tomatoes so that both are produced on the same plant, one above ground and one underground.
  - Cacti of widely different forms are sometimes grafted on to each other.
  - Multiple cultivars of fruits such as apples are sometimes grafted on a single tree. This so-called “family tree” provides more fruit variety for small spaces such as a suburban backyard, and also takes care of the need for pollenizers. The

drawback is that the gardener must be sufficiently trained to prune them correctly, or one strong variety will usually "take over". Occasionally, a so-called "graft hybrid" or "chimaera" can occur where the tissues of the stock continue to grow within the scion. Such a plant can produce flowers and foliage typical of both plants as well as shoots intermediate between the two. The best-known example is probably +*Laburnocytisus* 'Adamii', a graft hybrid between laburnum and broom, which originated in a nursery near Paris, France in 1825. This small tree bears yellow flowers typical of *Laburnum anagyroides*, purple flowers typical of *Chamaecytisus purpureus* and curious coppery-pink flowers which show characteristics of both "parents".

- Ornamental and functional, tree shaping uses grafting techniques to join separate trees or parts of the same tree to itself. Furniture, hearts, entry archways are examples. Axel Erlandson was a prolific tree shaper growing over 75 mature shaped and grafted trees.

Techniques

Approach

Approach grafting or inarching is used to join plants that are otherwise difficult to join. The plants are grown close together, and then joined so that each plant has roots below and growth above the point of union. Both scion and stock retain their respective parents that may or may not be removed after joining. Also used in pleaching. The graft can be successfully accomplished any time of year.

Budding

Grafting with a single eye or bud. Normally performed at the height of the growing season by inserting a dormant bud into a shallow slice under the rind of the tree. The bud is sealed from drying and bound in place. There are many styles of budding depending on the cutting and fitting methods, the most popular being shield budding.

Other budding styles include the inverted T, patch budding, double shield, flute budding and chip budding.

Cleft

The most common form of grafting is cleft grafting. The stock is simply split and the scion is inserted. It is best if the stock is 2-7 cm in diameter and has 3-5 buds, and the cleft is around 7cm deep. is cut in a wedge shape and inserted into the tree with the cambium. The bare stock is covered with grafting compound, otherwise the cambium layer quickly dries and the graft fails.

Stub

Stub grafting is a technique that requires less stock than cleft grafting, and retains the shape of a tree. Also scions are generally of 6-8 buds in this process.

An incision is made into the branch one centimetre long, then the scion is wedged and forced into the branch. The scion should be at an angle of at most 35° to the parent tree so that the crotch remains strong. The graft is covered with grafting compound.

Awl

Awl grafting takes the least resources and the least time. It is best done by an experienced grafter, as it is possible to accidentally drive the tool too far into the stock, reducing the scion's chance of survival. Awl grafting can be done by using a screwdriver to make a slit in the bark, not penetrating the cambium layer completely. Then inset the wedged scion into the incision.

Veneer

Veneer grafting, or inlay grafting, is a method used for stocks larger than three centimeters in diameter. The scion is recommended to be about as thick as a pencil. Clefts are made of the same size as the scion on the side of the branch, not on top. The scion end is shaped as a wedge, inserted, and wrapped with tape to the scaffolding branches to give it more strength.

Renewing Fusion

"Renewing fusion" is a grafting method in which a small branch (at least a centimeter wide) from one plant to a main branch of another, by carefully shaving a proper amount of bark from the large branch and inserting the scion into a cut hole. The graft is taped with a thin strip of duct tape in diagonal lashings, to hold it up and to prevent insects from entering the hole.

Natural Grafting

Tree branches and more often roots of the same species will sometimes naturally graft, this is called inosculation. When roots make physical contact with each other they often grow together. A group of trees can share water and mineral nutrients via root grafts, which may be advantageous to weaker trees, and may also form a larger rootmass as an adaptation to promote fire resistance and regeneration as exemplified by the California Black Oak.

A problem with root grafts is that they allow transmission of certain pathogens, such as Dutch elm disease. Inosculation also sometimes occurs where two stems on the same tree, shrub or vine make contact with each other. This is common in plants such as strawberries and potatoes.

Scientific Uses

Grafting has been important in flowering research. Leaves or shoots from plants induced to flower can be grafted onto uninduced plants and transmit a floral stimulus that induces them to flower.

The transmission of plant viruses has been studied using grafting. Virus indexing involves grafting a symptomless plant that is suspected of carrying a virus onto an indicator plant that is very susceptible to the virus.

Herbaceous Grafting

Grafting is often done for non-woody plants such as a tomato, cucumber, eggplant and watermelon. The main advantage of grafting is for disease-resistant rootstocks. In Japan there is an automated process using grafting robots.

Plant Hormone

Plant hormones (also known as phytohormones) are chemicals that regulate plant growth. Plant hormones are signal molecules produced within the plant, and occur in extremely low concentrations. Hormones regulate cellular processes in targeted cells locally and when moved to other locations, in other locations of the plant. Hormones also determine the formation of flowers, stems, leaves, the shedding of leaves, and the development and ripening of fruit. Plants, unlike animals, lack glands that produce and secrete hormones. Plant hormones shape the plant, affecting seed growth, time of flowering, the sex of flowers, senescence of leaves and fruits. They affect which tissues grow upward and which grow downward, leaf formation and stem growth, fruit development and ripening, plant longevity and even plant death. Hormones are vital to plant growth and lacking them, plants would be mostly a mass of undifferentiated cells.

Characteristics

The word hormone is derived from Greek and means 'set in motion'. Plant hormones affect gene expression and transcription levels, cellular division and growth. They are naturally produced within plants, though very similar chemicals are produced by fungi and bacteria that can also effect plant growth a large number of related chemical compounds are synthesized by humans, they are used to regulate the growth of cultivated plants, weeds, and in vitro grown plants and plant cells; these man made compounds are called Plant Growth Regulators or PGRs for short. Early in the study of plant hormones, "phytohormone" was the commonly-used term, but its use is less widely applied now.

Plant hormones are not nutrients, but chemicals that in small amounts promote and influence the growth, development, and differentiation of cells and tissues. The biosynthesis of plant hormones within plant tissues is often diffuse and not always localized. Plants lack glands to produce and store hormones, because, unlike animals, which have two circulatory systems (lymphatic and cardiovascular) powered by a heart that moves fluids around the body, plants use more passive means to move chemicals around the plant. Plants utilize simple chemicals as hormones, which move more easily through the plant's tissues. They are often produced and used on a local basis within the plant body, plant cells even produce hormones that affect different regions of the cell producing the hormone.

Hormones are transported within the plant by utilizing four types of movements. For localized movement, cytoplasmic streaming within cells and slow diffusion of ions and molecules between cells are utilized. Vascular tissues are used to move hormones from one part of the plant to another; these include sieve tubes that move sugars from the leaves to the roots and flowers, and xylem that moves water and mineral solutes from the roots to the foliage.

Not all plant cells respond to hormones, but those cells that do are programmed to respond at specific points in their growth cycle. The greatest effects occur at specific stages during the cell's life, with diminished effects occurring before or after this period. Plants need hormones at very specific times during plant growth and at specific locations. They also need to disengage the effects that hormones have when they are no longer needed. The production of hormones occurs very often at sites of active growth within the meristems, before cells have fully differentiated. After production they are sometimes moved to other parts of the plant where they cause an immediate effect or they can be stored in cells to be released later. Plants use different pathways to regulate internal hormone quantities and moderate their effects; they can regulate the amount of chemicals used to biosynthesize hormones. They can store them in cells, inactivate them, or cannibalise already-formed hormones by conjugating them with carbohydrates, amino acids or peptides. Plants can also break down hormones chemically, effectively destroying them. Plants also move hormones around the plant diluting their concentrations.

The concentration of hormones required for plant responses are very low (10-6 to 10-5 mol/L). Because of these low concentrations it has been very difficult to study plant hormones and only since the late 1970s have scientists been able to start piecing together their effects and relationships to plant physiology. Much of the early work on plant hormones involved studying plants that were genetically deficient in one or involved the use of tissue cultured plants grown *in vitro* that were subjected to differing ratios of hormones and the resultant growth compared. The earliest scientific observation and study dates to the 1880s; the determination and observation of plant hormones and their identification was spread-out over the next 70 years.

Classes of Plant Hormones

It is generally accepted that there are five major classes of plant hormones, some of which are made up of many different chemicals that can vary in structure from one plant to the next. The chemicals are each grouped together into one of these classes based on their structural similarities and on their effects on plant physiology. Other plant hormones and growth regulators are not easily grouped into these classes, they exist naturally or are synthesized by humans or other organisms, including chemicals that inhibit plant growth or interrupt the physiological processes within plants. Each class has positive as well as inhibitory functions, and most often work in tandem with each other, with varying ratios of one or more interplaying to affect growth regulation.

Abscisic Acid

Abscisic acid also called ABA, was discovered and researched under two different names before its chemical properties were fully known, it was called *dormin* and *abscicin II*. Once it was determined that the two latter named compounds were the same, it was named abscisic acid. The name "abscisic acid" was given because it was found in high concentrations in newly-abscissed or freshly-fallen leaves.

This class of PGR is composed of one chemical compound normally produced in the leaves of plants, originating from chloroplasts, especially when plants are under stress. In general, it acts as an inhibitory chemical compound that affects bud growth, seed and bud dormancy. It mediates changes within the apical meristem causing bud dormancy and the alteration of the last set of leaves into protective bud covers. Since it was found in freshly-abscissed leaves, it was thought to play a role in the processes of natural leaf drop but further research has disproven this. In plant species from temperate parts of the world it plays a role in leaf and seed dormancy by inhibiting growth, but, as it is dissipated from seeds or buds, growth begins. In other plants, as ABA levels decrease, growth then commences as gibberellin levels increase. Without ABA, buds and seeds would start to grow during warm periods in winter and be killed when it froze again. Since ABA dissipates slowly from the tissues and its effects take time to be offset by other plant hormones, there is a delay in physiological pathways that provide some protection from premature growth. It accumulates within seeds during fruit maturation, preventing seed germination within the fruit, or seed germination before winter. Abscisic acid's effects are degraded within plant tissues during cold temperatures or by its removal by water washing in out of the tissues, releasing the seeds and buds from dormancy.

In plants under water stress ABA plays a role in closing the stomata. Soon after plants are water stressed and the roots are deficient in water, a signal moves up to the leaves causing the formation of ABA precursors there which then move to the roots. The roots then release ABA which is translocated to the foliage through the vascular system and modulates the potassium and sodium uptake within the guard cells, which then lose turgidity, closing the stomata ABA exists in all parts of the plant and its concentration within any tissue seems to mediate its effects and function as a hormone, its degradation or more properly catabolism within the plant affects metabolic reactions and cellular growth and production of other hormones Plants start life as a seed with high ABA levels, just before the seed germinates ABA levels decrease; during germination and early growth of the seedling, ABA levels decrease even more. As plants begin to produce shoots with fully functional leaves - ABA levels begin to increase, slowing down cellular growth in more "mature" areas of the plant. Stress from water or predation affects ABA production and catabolism rates which mediate another cascade of effects triggering specific responses from targeted cells. Scientists are still piecing together the complex interactions and effects of this and other phytohormones.

Auxins

Auxins are compounds that positively influence cell enlargement, bud formation and root initiation. They also promote the production of other hormones and in conjunction with cytokinins, they control the growth of stems, roots, flowers and fruits. Auxins were the first class of growth regulators discovered. They affect cell elongation by altering cell wall plasticity. Auxins decrease in light and increase where its dark. They stimulate cambium cells to divide and in stems cause secondary xylem to differentiate. Auxins act to inhibit the growth of buds lower down the stems (apical dominance), and also to promote lateral and adventitious root development and growth. Auxins promote flower initiation, converting stems into flowers. Leaf abscission is initiated by the growing point of a plant ceasing to produce auxins. Auxins in seeds regulate specific protein synthesis as they develop within the flower after pollination, causing the flower to develop a fruit to contain the developing seeds. Auxins are toxic to plants in large concentrations; they are most toxic to dicots and less so to monocots. Because of this property, synthetic auxin herbicides including 2, 4-D and 2, 4, 5-T have been developed and used for weed control. Auxins, especially 1-Naphthaleneacetic acid (NAA) and Indole-3-butyric acid (IBA), are also commonly applied to stimulate root growth when taking cuttings of plants. The most common auxin found in plants is indoleacetic acid or IAA.

Cytokinins

Cytokinins or CKs are a group of chemicals that influence cell division and shoot formation. They were called kinins in the past when the first cytokinins were isolated from yeast cells. They also help delay senescence or the aging of tissues, are responsible for mediating auxin transport throughout the plant, and affect internodal length and leaf growth. They have a highly-synergistic effect in concert with auxins and the ratios of these two groups of plant hormones affect most major growth periods during a plant's lifetime. Cytokinins counter the apical dominance induced by auxins; they in conjunction with ethylene promote abscission of leaves, flower parts and fruits.

Ethylene

Ethylene is a gas that forms through the Yang Cycle from the breakdown of methionine, which is in all cells. Ethylene has very limited solubility in water and does not accumulate within the cell but diffuses out of the cell and escapes out of the plant. Its effectiveness as a plant hormone is dependent on its rate of production versus its rate of escaping into the atmosphere. Ethylene is produced at a faster rate in rapidly growing and dividing cells, especially in darkness. New growth and newly-germinated seedlings produce more ethylene than can escape the plant, which leads to elevated amounts of ethylene, inhibiting leaf expansion. As the new shoot is exposed to light, reactions by phytochrome in the plant's cells produce a signal for ethylene production to decrease, allowing leaf expansion. Ethylene affects cell growth and cell shape; when a growing shoot hits an obstacle while underground, ethylene production greatly increases, preventing cell elongation and causing the stem to swell. The resulting thicker stem can exert more pressure against the object impeding its path to the surface. If the shoot does not reach the surface and the ethylene stimulus becomes prolonged, it affects the stems natural geotropic response, which is to grow upright, allowing it to grow around an object. Studies seem to indicate that ethylene affects stem diameter and height: When stems of trees are subjected to wind, causing lateral stress, greater ethylene production occurs, resulting in thicker, more sturdy tree trunks and branches. Ethylene affects fruit-ripening: Normally, when the seeds are mature, ethylene production increases and builds-up within the fruit, resulting in a climacteric event just before seed dispersal. The nuclear protein Ethylene Insensitive2 (EIN2) is regulated by ethylene production, and, in turn, regulates other hormones including ABA and stress hormones.

Gibberellins

Gibberellins or GAs include a large range of chemicals that are produced naturally within plants and by fungi. They were first discovered when Japanese researchers, including Eiichi Kurosawa, noticed a chemical produced by a fungus called *Gibberella fujikuroi* that produced abnormal growth in rice plants. Gibberellins are important in seed germination, affecting enzyme production which mobilizes food production used for growth of new cells. This is done by modulating chromosomal transcription. In grain (rice, wheat, corn, etc.) seeds, a layer of cells called the aleurone layer wraps around the endosperm tissue. Absoption of water by the seed causes production of GA. The GA is transported to the aleurone layer, which responds by producing enzymes that break down stored food reserves within the endosperm, which are utilized by the growing seedling. GAs produce bolting of rosette-forming plants, increasing internodal length. They promote flowering, cellular division, and in seeds growth after germination. Gibberellins also reverse the inhibition of shoot growth and dormancy induced by ABA.

Other Known Hormones

Other identified plant growth regulators include:

- **Brassinolides** - plant steroids that are chemically similar to animal steroid hormones. First isolated from pollen of the mustard family and extensively studied in *Arabidopsis*. They promote cell elongation and cell division, differentiation of xylem tissues, and inhibit leaf abscission. Plants that are deficient in brassinolides suffer from dwarfism.

- **Salicylic acid** - activates genes in some plants that produce chemicals that aid in the defense against pathogenic invaders.
- **Jasmonates** - are produced from fatty acids and seem to promote the production of defense proteins that are used to fend off invading organisms. They are believed to also have a role in seed germination, and affect the storage of protein in seeds, and seem to affect root growth.
- **Plant peptide hormones** - encompass all small secreted peptides that are involved in cell-to-cell signaling. These small peptide hormones play crucial roles in plant growth and development, including defense mechanisms, the control of cell division and expansion, and pollen self-incompatibility.
- **Polyamines** - are strongly basic molecules with low molecular weight that have been found in all organisms studied thus far. They are essential for plant growth and development and affect the process of mitosis and meiosis.
- **Nitric oxide** (NO) - serves as signal in hormonal and defense responses.
- **Strigolactones**, implicated in the inhibition of shoot branching.

Potential Medical Applications

Plant stress hormones activate cellular responses, including cell death, to diverse stress situations in plants. Researchers have found that some plant stress hormones share the ability to adversely affect human cancer cells . For example, sodium salicylate has been found to suppress proliferation of lymphoblastic leukemia, prostate, breast, and melanoma human cancer cells. Jasmonic acid, a plant stress hormone that belongs to the jasmonate family, induced death in lymphoblastic leukemia cells. Methyl jasmonate has been found to induce cell death in a number of cancer cell lines.

Hormones and Plant Propagation

Synthetic plant hormones or PGRs are commonly used in a number of different techniques involving plant propagation from cuttings, grafting, micropropagation, and tissue culture. The propagation of plants by cuttings of fully-developed leaves, stems, or roots is performed by gardeners utilizing auxin as a rooting compound applied to the cut surface; the auxins are taken into the plant and promote root initiation. In grafting, auxin promotes callus tissue formation, which joins the surfaces of the graft together. In micropropagation, different PGRs are used to promote multiplication and then rooting of new plantlets. In the tissue-culturing of plant cells, PGRs are used to produce callus growth, multiplication, and rooting.

Seed Dormancy

Plant hormones affect seed germination and dormancy by affecting different parts of the seed. Embryo dormancy is characterized by a high ABA/GA ratio, whereas the seed has a high ABA sensitivity and low GA sensitivity. To release the seed from this type of dormancy and initiate seed germination, an alteration in hormone biosynthesis and degradation towards a low ABA/GA ratio, along with a decrease in ABA sensitivity and an increase in GA sensitivity needs to occur. ABA controls embryo dormancy, and GA embryo germination. Seed coat dormancy involves the mechanical restriction of the seed coat, this along with a low embryo growth potential, effectively produces seed dormancy. GA releases this dormancy by increasing the embryo growth potential, and/or weakening the seed coat so the radical of the seedling can break through the seed coat. Different types of seed coats can be made up of living or dead cells and both types can be influenced by hormones;

those composed of living cells are acted upon after seed formation while the seed coats composed of dead cells can be influenced by hormones during the formation of the seed coat. ABA affects testa or seed coat growth characteristics, including thickness, and effects the GA-mediated embryo growth potential. These conditions and effects occur during the formation of the seed, often in response to environmental conditions. Hormones also mediate endosperm dormancy: Endosperm in most seeds is composed of living tissue that can actively respond to hormones generated by the embryo. The endosperm often acts as a barrier to seed germination, playing a part in seed coat dormancy or in the germination process. Living cells respond to and also affect the ABA/GA ratio, and mediate cellular sensitivity; GA thus increases the embryo growth potential and can promote endosperm weakening. GA also affects both ABA-independent and ABA-inhibiting processes within the endosperm.

Cell Membranes

One universal feature of all cells is an outer limiting membrane called the plasma membrane. In addition, all eukaryotic cells contain elaborate systems of internal membranes which set up various membrane-enclosed compartments within the cell. Cell membranes are built from lipids and proteins.

The Plasma Membrane

The plasma membrane serves as the interface between the machinery in the interior of the cell and the extracellular fluid (ECF) that bathes all cells.

The lipids in the plasma membrane are chiefly phospholipids like phosphatidyl ethanolamine and cholesterol. Phospholipids are amphiphilic with the hydrocarbon tail of the molecule being hydrophobic; its polar head hydrophilic. As the plasma membrane faces watery solutions on both sides, its phospholipids accommodate this by forming a phospholipid bilayer with the hydrophobic tails facing each other.

Integral Membrane Proteins

Many of the proteins associated with the plasma membrane are tightly bound to it.

- Some are attached to lipids in the bilayer.
- In others - the transmembrane proteins - the polypeptide chain actually traverses the lipid bilayer. The figure shows a transmembrane protein that passes just once through the bilayer and another that passes through it 7 times. All G-protein-coupled receptors (e.g., receptors of peptide hormones, and odors each span the plasma membrane 7 times.

In all these cases, the portion within the lipid bilayer consists primarily of hydrophobic amino acids. These are usually arranged in an alpha helix so that the polar -C=O and -NH groups at the peptide bonds can interact with each other rather than with their hydrophobic surroundings.

Those portions of the polypeptide that project out from the bilayer tend to have a high percentage of hydrophilic amino acids. Furthermore, those that project into the aqueous surroundings of the cell are usually glycoproteins, with many hydrophilic sugar residues attached to the part of the polypeptide exposed at the surface of the cell.

Some transmembrane proteins that span the bilayer several times form a hydrophilic channel through which certain ions and molecules can enter (or leave) the cell.

Peripheral Membrane Proteins

These are more loosely associated with the membrane. They are usually attached noncovalently to the protruding portions of integral membrane proteins. Membrane proteins are often restricted in their movements.

A lipid bilayer is really a film of oil. Thus we might expect that structures immersed in it would be relatively free to float about. For some membrane proteins, this is the case. For others, however, their mobility is limited:

- Some of the proteins exposed at the interior face of the plasma membrane are tethered to cytoskeletal elements like actin microfilaments.

- Some proteins are the exterior face of the plasma membrane are anchored to components of the extracellular matrix like collagen.
- Integral membrane proteins cannot pass through the tight junctions found between some kinds of cells (e.g., epithelial cells).

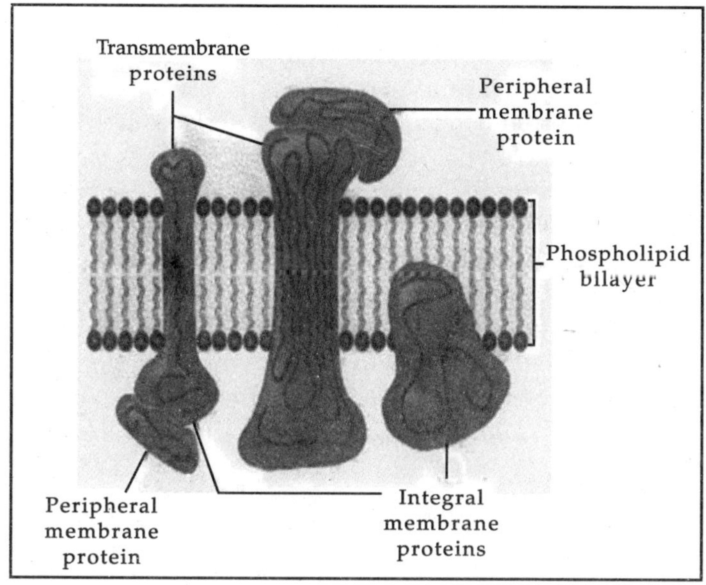

Fig. 7.1

THE NUCLEUS

The nucleus is the hallmark of eukaryotic cells; the very term eukaryotic means having a "true nucleus".

The Nuclear Envelope

The nucleus is enveloped by a pair of membranes enclosing a lumen that is continuous with that of the endoplasmic reticulum. The inner membrane is stabilized by a meshwork of intermediate filament proteins called lamins.

The nuclear envelope is perforated by thousands of nuclear pore complexes (NPCs) that control the passage of molecules in and out of the nucleus.

Chromatin

The nucleus contains the chromosomes of the cell. Each chromosome consists of a single molecule of DNA complexed with an equal mass of proteins. Collectively, the DNA of the nucleus with its associated proteins is called chromatin. Most of the protein consists of multiple copies of 5 kinds of histones. These are basic proteins, bristling with positively charged arginine and lysine residues. (Both Arg and Lys have a free amino group on their R group, which attracts protons (H^+) giving them a positive charge.) Just the choice of amino acids you would make to bind tightly to the negatively-charged phosphate groups of DNA. Chromatin also contains small amounts of a wide variety of nonhistone proteins. Most of these are transcription factors (e.g., the steroid receptors) and their association with the DNA is more transient.

Nucleosomes

Two copies of each of four kinds of histones:

- H2A;
- H2B;
- H3 and
- H4.

form a core of protein, the nucleosome core. Around this is wrapped about 147 base pairs of DNA.

From 20-60 bp of DNA link one nucleosome to the next. Each linker region is occupied by a single molecule of histone 1 (H1).

The binding of histones to DNA does not depend on particular nucleotide sequences in the DNA but does depend critically on the amino acid sequence of the histone. Histones are some of the most conserved molecules during the course of evolution. Histone H_4 in the calf differs from H4 in the pea plant at only two amino acids residues in the chain of 102.

The formation of nucleosomes helps somewhat, but not nearly enough, to make the DNA sufficiently compact to fit in the nucleus. In order to fit 46 DNA molecules (in humans), totaling over 2 meters in length, into a nucleus that may be only 10 µm across requires more extensive folding and compaction.

- Interactions between the exposed "tails" of the core histones causes nucleosomes to associate into a compact fiber 30 nm in diameter.
- These fibers are then folded into more complex structures whose precise configuration is uncertain and which probably changes with the level of activity of the genes in the region.

Histone Modifications

Although their amino acid sequence (primary structure) is unvarying, individual histone molecules do vary in structure as a result of chemical modifications that occur later to individual amino acids.

These include adding:

- acetyl groups (CH_3CO^-) to lysines
- phosphate groups to serines and threonines
- methyl groups to lysines and arginines

Although 75-80% of the histone molecule is incorporated in the core, the remainder—at the N-terminal—dangles out from the core as a "tail".

The chemical modifications occur on these tails, especially of H_3 and H_4. Most of theses changes are reversible. For example, acetyl groups are:

- added by enzymes called histone acetyltransferases (HATs) (not to be confused with the "HAT" medium used to make monoclonal antibodies!); and
- removed by histone deacetylases (HDACs).

More often than not, acetylation of histone tails occurs in regions of chromatin that become active in gene transcription. This makes a kind of intuitive sense as adding acetyl groups neutralizes the positive charges on Lys thus reducing the strength of the association between the highly-negative DNA and the highly-positive histones.

But there is surely more to the story.

- Acetylation of Lys-16 on H_4 ("H_4 K16ac") prevents the interaction of their "tails" needed to form the compact 30-nm structure of inactive chromatin and thus is associated with active genes. Note that this case involves interrupting protein-protein not protein-DNA interactions.
- Methylation, which also neutralizes the charge on lysines (and arginines), can either stimulate or inhibit gene transcription in that region.
  - Methylation of lysine-4 in H3 ("H_3 K_4me") is associated with active genes while.
  - methylation of lysine-9 and/or lysine-27 in H_3 (H_3K_9me and H_3K_{27}me respectively) is associated with inactive genes. (These include those imprinted genes that have been permanently inactivated in somatic cells.
- And adding phosphates causes the chromosomes to become more — not less — compact as they get ready for mitosis and meiosis.

In any case, it is now clear that histones are a dynamic component of chromatin and not simply inert DNA-packing material.

Histone Variants

- We have genes for 8 different varieties of histone 1 (H1). Which variety is found at a particular linker depends on such factors:
  - the type of cell;
  - where it is in the cell cycle; and
  - its stage of differentiation.

In some cases, at least, a particular variant of H1 associates with certain transcription factors to bind to the enhancer of specific genes turning off expression of those genes.

Some other examples of histone variants:

- H3 is replaced by CENP-A ("centromere protein A") at the nucleosomes near centromeres. Failure to substitute CENP-A for H3 in this regions blocks centromere structure and function.
- H2A may be replaced by the variant H2A.Z at the boundaries between euchromatin and heterochromatin.
- All the "standard" histones are replaced by variants as sperm develop.

In general, the "standard" histones are incorporated into the nucleosomes as new DNA is synthesized during S phase of the cell cycle. Later, some are replaced by variant histones as conditions in the cell dictate.

Chromosome Territories

During interphase, little can be seen of chromatin structure (except for special cases like the polytene chromosomes of Drosophila and some other flies). Although each chromosome is greatly elongated, it tends to occupy a discrete region within the nucleus called its territory. This can be demonstrated by:

- directing a tiny laser beam at a small portion of the nucleus. If all the chromsomes were intertwined, one would expect that all would receive some damage. That does not occur—only one or two chromosomes are damaged.
- Fluorescent stains specific for a particular chromosome stain only two regions in the nucleus — revealing the territory of the two homologs.

"Kissing" Chromosomes

Portions of one chromosome can loop out of its territory and interact with part of a different chromosome looping out from its territory. These are "kissing" chromosomes.

The examples that have been found so far indicate that these interactions are another way of coordinating the activity of genes residing on different chromosomes.

Example

The human genome contains many genes — scattered along different chromosomes — that are turned on by the arrival of a single signal. Among the many genes activated by estrogen, are *TIFF1* on chromosome 21 and *GREB1* on chromosome 2. Using FISH analysis, researchers at the University of California in San Diego showed that within a little as 2 minutes after exposing cells to estrogen, the *TIFF1* and *GREB1* loci move from their respective chromosome territories and "kiss".

Another Example

In the mouse, naive helper T cells — awaiting a signal to direct them to become either Th1 cells or Th2 cells— have:

- the part of chromosome 10 carrying the gene for interferon-gamma (a Th1 cytokine) kissing.
- the part of chromosome 11 carrying the genes for IL-4 and IL-5 (Th2 cytokines).

When the cell receives the signals committing it to one path or the other, the two regions separate, the appropriate one going to a region of active transcription; the other to a region of heterochromatin.

Euchromatin versus Heterochromatin

The density of the chromatin that makes up each chromosome (that is, how tightly it is packed) varies along the length of the chromosome.

- dense regions are called heterochromatin
- less dense regions are called euchromatin.

Heterochromatin

Heterochromatin is found in parts of the chromosome where there are few or no genes, such as:

- centromeres;
  - telomeres;
  - is densely-packed;
- is greatly enriched with transposons and other "junk" DNA;
- is replicated late in S phase of the cell cycle;
- has reduced crossing over in meiosis; and
- Those genes present in heterochromatin are generally inactive; that is, not transcribed and show.
  - *increased methylation* of the cytosines in CpG islands of the DNA.
  - *decreased acetylation* of histones; and
  - *increased methylation* of lysine-9 in histone H3, which now provides a binding site for heterochromatin protein 1 (HP1), which blocks access by the transcription factors needed for gene transcription.

- *increased methylation* of lysine-27 in histone H_3 (H_3K_{27}).

Euchromatin

- It is found in parts of the chromosome that contain many genes;
- It is loosely-packed in loops of 30-nm fibers.
- These are separated from adjacent heterochromatin by insulators.

In yeast, the loops are often found near the *nuclear pore complexes*. This would seem to make sense making it easier for the gene transcripts to get to the cytosol. However, in animal cells, gene transcription appears to be repressed near the inner surface of the nuclear envelope.

- The genes in euchromatin are active and thus show.
  - decreased methylation of the cytosines in CpG islands of the DNA.
  - increased acetylation of histones; and
  - decreased methylation of lysine-9 and lysine-27 in histone H3.

Nucleosomes and Transcription

Transcription factors cannot bind to their promoter if the promoter is blocked by a nucleosome. One of the first functions of the assembling transcription factors is to either expel the nucleosome from the site where transcription begins or at least to slide the nucleosomes along the DNA molecule. Either action exposes the gene's promoter so that the transcription factors can then bind to it.

The actual transcription of protein-coding genes is done by RNA polymerase II (RNAP II). In order for it to travel along the DNA to be transcribed, a complex of proteins removes the nucleosomes in front of it and then replaces them after RNAP II has transcribed that portion of DNA and moved on.

The Nucleolus

During the period between cell divisions, when the chromosomes are in their extended state, 1 or more of them (10 in human cells) have loops extending into a spherical mass called the nucleolus. Here are synthesized three (of the four) kinds of RNA molecules (28S, 18S, 5.8S) used in the assembly of the large and small subunits of ribosomes.

28S, 18S, and 5.8S ribosomal RNA is transcribed (by RNA polymerase I) from hundreds to thousands of tandemly-arranged rDNA genes distributed (in humans) on 10 different chromosomes. The rDNA-containing regions of these 10 chromosomes cluster together in the nucleolus.

(In yeast, the 5S rRNA molecules — as well as transfer RNA molecules — are also synthesized (by RNA polymerase III) in the nucleolus.)

Once formed, rRNA molecules associate with the dozens of different ribosomal proteins used in the assembly of the large and small subunits of the ribosome. But all proteins are synthesized in the cytosol — and all the ribosomes are needed in the cytosol to do their work — so there must be a mechanism for the transport of these large structures in and out of the nucleus. This is one of the functions of the nuclear pore complexes.

Nuclear Pore Complexes (NPCs)

The entire assembly forms an aqueous channel connecting the cytosol with the interior of the nucleus ("nucleoplasm"). When materials are to be transported through the pore, it opens up to form a channel some 25 nm wide — large enough to get such large assemblies as ribosomal subunits through.

Transport through the nuclear pore complexes is active; that is, it requires:

- energy

- many different carrier molecules each specialized to transport a particular cargo
- docking molecules in the NPC (represented here as colored rods and disks)

Import into the Nucleus

All proteins are synthesized in the cytosol and those needed by the nucleus must be imported into it through the NPCs. Probably each of these proteins has a characteristic sequence of amino acids — called a nuclear localization sequence (NLS) — that targets it for entry.

They include:

- all the *histones* needed to make the nucleosomes;
- all the *ribosomal proteins* needed for the assembly of ribosomes;
- all the *transcription* factors (e.g., the steroid receptors) needed to turn genes on (and off);
- all the *splicing factors* needed to process pre-mRNA into mature mRNA molecules; that is, to cut out intron regions and splice the exon regions.

Export from the Nucleus

Molecules and macromolecular assemblies exported from the nucleus include:

- the *ribosomal subunits* containing both rRNA and proteins
- *messenger RNA* (mRNA) molecules (accompanied by proteins)
- *transfer RNA* (tRNA) molecules (also accompanied by proteins)
- *transcription factors* that are returned to the cytosol to await reuse

Both the RNA and protein molecules contain a characteristic nuclear export sequence (NES) needed to ensure their association with the right carrier molecules to take them out to the cytosol.

Nucleoplasm

The term "nucleoplasm" is still used to describe the contents of the nucleus. However, the term disguises the structural complexity and order that seems to exist within the nucleus. For example, there is evidence that DNA replication and transcription occur at discrete sites within the nucleus.

CELLULAR RESPIRATION

Cellular respiration is the process of oxidizing food molecules, like glucose, to carbon dioxide and water. The energy released is trapped in the form of ATP (Adenosine triphosphate) for use by all the energy-consuming activities of the cell.

The process occurs in two phases:

- glycolysis, the breakdown of glucose to pyruvic acid.
- the complete oxidation of pyruvic acid to carbon dioxide and water.

Mitochondria

Mitochondria are membrane-enclosed organelles distributed through the cytosol of most eukaryotic cells. Their number within the cell ranges from a few hundred to, in very active cells, thousands. Their main function is the conversion of the potential energy of food molecules into ATP. Mitochondria have:

- an outer membrane that encloses the entire structure
- an inner membrane that encloses a fluid-filled matrix
- between the two is the intermembrane space

- the inner membrane is elaborately folded with shelflike cristae projecting into the matrix.
- a small number (some 5-10) circular molecules of DNA

The number of mitochondria in a cell can:

- increase by their fission (e.g. following mitosis);
- decrease by their fusing together.

The Outer Membrane

The outer membrane contains many complexes of integral membrane proteins that form channels through which a variety of molecules and ions move in and out of the mitochondrion.

The Inner Membrane

The inner membrane contains 5 complexes of integral membrane proteins:

- NADH dehydrogenase (Complex I)
- succinate dehydrogenase (Complex II)
- cytochrome c reductase (Complex III; also known as the cytochrome b-c1 complex)
- cytochrome c oxidase (Complex IV)
- ATP synthase (Complex V)

The Matrix

The matrix contains a complex mixture of soluble enzymes that catalyze the respiration of pyruvic acid and other small organic molecules.

Here pyruvic acid is:

- oxidized by NAD+ producing NADH + H+
- decarboxylated producing a molecule of:
  - carbon dioxide (CO_2); and
  - a 2-carbon fragment of acetate bound to coenzyme A forming acetyl-CoA

The Citric Acid Cycle

- This 2-carbon fragment is donated to a molecule of *oxaloacetic acid.*
- The resulting molecule of *citric acid* (which gives its name to the process) undergoes the series of enzymatic steps shown in the diagram.
- The final step regenerates a molecule of oxaloacetic acid and the cycle is ready to turn again.

Summary

- Each of the 3 carbon atoms present in the pyruvate that entered the mitochondrion leaves as a molecule of carbon dioxide (CO_2).
- At 4 steps, a pair of electrons ($2e^-$) is removed and transferred to NAD^+ reducing it to NADH + H^+.
- At one step, a pair of electrons is removed from succinic acid and reduces FAD to FADH2.

The electrons of NADH and FADH2 are transferred to the electron transport chain.

The Electron Transport Chain

The electron transport chain consists of 3 complexes of integral membrane proteins

- the NADH dehydrogenase complex (I)
- the cytochrome c reductase complex (III)
- the cytochrome c oxidase complex (IV) and two freely-diffusible molecules
- ubiquinone
- cytochrome c

that shuttle electrons from one complex to the next.

The electron transport chain accomplishes:

- the stepwise transfer of electrons from NADH (and $FADH_2$) to oxygen molecules to form (with the aid of protons) water molecules (H_2O);
- (Cytochrome c can only transfer one electron at a time, so cytochrome c oxidase must wait until it has accumulated 4 of them before it can react with oxygen.)
- harnessing the energy released by this transfer to the pumping of protons (H+) from the matrix to the intermembrane space.
- Approximately 20 protons are pumped into the intermembrane space as the 4 electrons needed to reduce oxygen to water pass through the respiratory chain.
- The gradient of protons formed across the inner membrane by this process of active transport forms a miniature battery.
- The protons can flow back down this gradient, reentering the matrix, only through another complex of integral proteins in the inner membrane, the ATP synthase complex.

Chemiosmosis in Mitochondria

The energy released as electrons pass down the gradient from NADH to oxygen is harnessed by three enzyme complexes of the respiratory chain (I, III, and IV) to pump protons (H^+) against their concentration gradient from the matrix of the mitochondrion into the intermembrane space (an example of active transport).

As their concentration increases there (which is the same as saying that the pH decreases), a strong diffusion gradient is set up. The only exit for these protons is through the ATP synthase complex. As in chloroplasts, the energy released as these protons flow down their gradient is harnessed to the synthesis of ATP. The process is called chemiosmosis and is an example of facilitated diffusion.

How many ATPs?

It is tempting to try to view the synthesis of ATP as a simple matter of stoichiometry (the fixed ratios of reactants to products in a chemical reaction). But (with 3 exceptions) it is not.

Most of the ATP is generated by the proton gradient that develops across the inner mitochondrial membrane. The number of protons pumped out as electrons drop from NADH through the respiratory chain to oxygen is theoretically large enough to generate, as they return through ATP synthase, 3 ATPs per electron pair (but only 2 ATPs for each pair donated by FADH2).

With 12 pairs of electrons removed from each glucose molecule.

- 10 by NAD^+ (so $10 \times 3 = 30$); and
- 2 by $FADH_2$ (so $2 \times 2 = 4$),

this could generate 34 ATPs.

Add to this the 4 ATPs that are generated by the 3 exceptions and one arrives at 38. But

- The energy stored in the proton gradient is also used for the active transport of several molecules and ions through the inner mitochondrial membrane into the matrix.
- NADH is also used as reducing agent for many cellular reactions.

So the actual yield of ATP as mitochondria respire varies with conditions. It probably seldom exceeds 30.

Three Exceptions

A stoichiometric production of ATP does occur at:

- one step in the citric acid cycle yielding 2 ATPs for each glucose molecule. This step is the conversion of alpha-ketoglutaric acid to succinic acid.

- at two steps in glycolysis yielding 2 ATPs for each glucose molecule.

Mitochondrial DNA (mtDNA)

The human mitochondrion contains 5-10 identical, circular molecules of DNA. Each consists of 16,569 base pairs carrying the information for 37 genes which encode:

- 2 different molecules of ribosomal RNA (rRNA)
- 22 different molecules of transfer RNA (tRNA) (at least one for each amino acid)
- 13 polypeptides.

The rRNA and tRNA molecules are used in the machinery that synthesizes the 13 polypeptides.

The 13 polypeptides participate in building several protein complexes embedded in the inner mitochondrial membrane.

- 7 subunits that make up the mitochondrial NADH dehydrogenase.
- 3 subunits of cytochrome c oxidase.
- 2 subunits of ATP synthase.
- cytochrome b.

Each of these protein complexes also requires subunits that are encoded by nuclear genes, synthesized in the cytosol, and imported from the cytosol into the mitochondrion. Nuclear genes also encode ~900 other proteins that must be imported into the mitochondrion.

Mutations in mtDNA Cause Human Diseases

A number of human diseases are caused by mutations in genes in our mitochondria:

- cytochrome b
- 12S rRNA

- ATP synthase
- subunits of NADH dehydrogenase
- several tRNA genes

Although many different organs may be affected, disorders of the muscles and brain are the most common. Perhaps this reflects the great demand for energy of both these organs. (Although representing only ~2% of our body weight, the brain consumes ~20% of the energy produced when we are at rest.)

Some of these disorders are inherited in the germline. In every case, the mutant gene is received from the mother because none of the mitochondria in sperm survives in the fertilized egg. Other disorders are somatic; that is, the mutation occurs in the somatic tissues of the individual.

Example: Exercise Intolerance

A number of humans who suffer from easily-fatigued muscles turn out to have a mutations in their cytochrome b gene. Curiously, only the mitochondria in their muscles have the mutation; the mtDNA of their other tissues is normal. Presumably, very early in their embryonic development, a mutation occurred in a cytochrome b gene in the mitochondrion of a cell destined to produce their muscles.

The severity of mitochondrial diseases varies greatly. The reason for this is probably the extensive mixing of mutant DNA and normal DNA in the mitochondria as they fuse with one another. A mixture of both is called heteroplasmy. The higher the ratio of mutant to normal, the greater the severity of the disease. In fact by chance alone, cells can on occasion end up with all their mitochondria carrying all-mutant genomes — a condition called homoplasmy (a phenomenon resembling genetic drift).

Why do mitochondria have their own genome?

Many of the features of the mitochondrial genetic system resemble those found in bacteria. This has strengthened the theory that mitochondria are the evolutionary descendants of a bacterium that established an endosymbiotic relationship with the ancestors of eukaryotic cells early in the history of life on earth. However, many of the genes needed for mitochondrial function have since moved to the nuclear genome.

THE CYTOSKELETON

Cells contain elaborate arrays of protein fibers that serve such functions as:

- establishing cell shape
- providing mechanical strength
- locomotion
- chromosome separation in mitosis and meiosis
- intracellular transport of organelles

The cytoskeleton is made up of three kinds of protein filaments:

- Actin filaments (also called microfilaments)
- Intermediate filaments and
- Microtubules

Actin Filaments

Monomers of the protein actin polymerize to form long, thin fibers. These are about 8 nm in diameter and, being the thinnest of the cytoskeletal filaments, are also called microfilaments. (In skeletal muscle fibers they are called "thin" filaments.) Some functions of actin filaments:

- form a band just beneath the plasma membrane:
  - provides mechanical strength to the cell

- links transmembrane proteins (e.g., cell surface receptors) to cytoplasmic proteins
- anchors the centrosomes at opposite poles of the cell during mitosis
- pinches dividing animal cells apart during cytokinesis

- generate cytoplasmic streaming in some cells
- generate locomotion in cells such as white blood cells and the amoeba
- interact with myosin ("thick") filaments in skeletal muscle fibers to provide the force of muscular contraction

Intermediate Filaments

These cytoplasmic fibers average 10 nm in diameter (and thus are "intermediate" in size between actin filaments (8 nm) and microtubules (25 nm) (as well as of the thick filaments of skeletal muscle fibers).

There are several types of intermediate filament, each constructed from one or more proteins characteristic of it.

- keratins are found in epithelial cells and also form hair and nails;
- nuclear lamins form a meshwork that stabilizes the inner membrane of the nuclear envelope;
- neurofilaments strengthen the long axons of neurons;
- vimentins provide mechanical strength to muscle (and other) cells.

Different kinds of epithelia use different keratins to build their intermediate filaments. Over 20 different kinds of keratins have been found, although each kind of epithelial cell may use no more than 2 of them. Up to 85% of the dry weight of squamous epithelial cells can consist of keratins.

Microtubules

- Microtubules;
- are straight, hollow cylinders whose wall is made up of a ring of 13 "protofilaments";
- have a diameter of about 25 nm;
- are variable in length but can grow 1000 times as long as they are wide;
- are built by the assembly of dimers of alpha tubulin and beta tubulin;
- are found in both animal and plant cells.

Microtubules

- grow at each end by the polymerization of tubulin dimers (powered by the hydrolysis of GTP); and
- shrink at each end by the release of tubulin dimers (depolymerization).

However, both processes always occur more rapidly at one end, called the plus end. The other, less active, end is the minus end.

Microtubules participate in a wide variety of cell activities. Most involve motion. The motion is provided by protein "motors" that use the energy of ATP to move along the microtubule.

Microtubule Motors

There are two major groups of microtubule motors:

- kinesins (most of these move toward the plus end of the microtubules); and
- dyneins (which move toward the minus end).

Some examples:

- The rapid transport of organelles, like vesicles and mitochondria, along the axons of neurons takes place along microtubules with their plus ends pointed toward the end of the axon. The motors are kinesins.

Charcot-Marie-Tooth disease. One cause of this rare disorder is an inherited mutated gene for one of the kinesins. In these patients, axonal transport is defective (which probably accounts for their muscle weakness first occurring in muscles at the ends of the longer motor neurons).

The migration of chromosomes in mitosis and meiosis takes place on microtubules that make up the spindle fibers. Both kinesins and dyneins are used as motors as we shall see below.

In plant cells, microtubules are created at many sites scattered through the cell. In animal cells, the microtubules originate at the centrosome.

CENTROSOME

The centrosome is:

- located in the cytoplasm attached to the outside of the nucleus.
- It is duplicated during S phase of the cell cycle.
- Just before mitosis, the two centrosomes move apart until they are on opposite sides of the nucleus.
- As mitosis proceeds, microtubules grow out from each centrosome with their plus ends growing toward the metaphase plate. These clusters of microtubules are called spindle fibers.

Spindle fibres have three destinations:

- Some attach to one kinetochore of a dyad with those growing from the opposite centrosome binding to the other kinetochore of that dyad.
- Some bind to the arms of the chromosomes.

- Still others continue growing from the two centrosomes until they extend between each other in a region of overlap.

All three groups of spindle fibers participate in:

- the assembly of the chromosomes at the metaphase plate at metaphase. Proposed mechanism (the diagram shows only 1 and 2).

1. Microtubules attached to opposite sides of the dyad shrink or grow until they are of equal length.
2. Microtubules motors attached to the kinetochores move them.
   - toward the minus end of shrinking microtubules (a dynein);
   - toward the plus end of lengthening microtubules (a kinesin).
3. The chromosome arms use a different kinesin to move to the metaphase plate.
   - the separation of the chromosomes at anaphase;
     - the sister kinetochores separate and, carrying their attached chromatid;
     - move along the microtubules powered by minus-end motors, dyneins, while the microtubules themselves shorten (probably at both ends);
   - the overlapping spindle fibers move past each other (pushing the poles farther apart) powered by plus-end motors, the "bipolar" kinesins; and
   - in this way the sister chromatids end up at opposite poles.

Other Functions of Centrosomes

In addition to their role in spindle formation, centrosomes play other important roles in animal cells:

- signaling that it is o.k. to proceed to cytokinesis. Destruction of both centrosomes with a laser beam prevents cytokinesis even if mitosis has been completed normally.
- signaling that it is o.k. for the daughter cells to begin another round of the cell cycle; specifically to duplicate their chromosomes in the next S phase. Destruction of one centrosome with a laser beam still permits cytokinesis but the daughter cells fail to enter a new S phase.
- Segregating signaling molecules (e.g., mRNAs) so that they pass into only one of the two daughter cells produced by mitosis. In this way, the two daughter cells can enter different pathways of differentiation even though they contain identical genomes.
- In at least some developing neurons, the position of the centrosome establishes the point at which the axon will grow out.

Centrosomes and Cancer

Cancer cells often have more than the normal number (1 or 2 depending on the stage of the cell cycle) of centrosomes. They also are aneuploid (have abnormal numbers of chromosomes), and considering the role of centrosomes in chromosome movement, it is tempting to think that the two phenomena are related.

Mutations in the tumor suppressor gene p53 seem to predispose the cell to excess replication of the centrosomes.

Chromosome movement in mitosis also involves polymerization and depolymerization of the microtubules. Taxol, a drug found in the bark of the Pacific yew, prevents depolymerization of the microtubules of the spindle fiber. This, in turn, stops chromosome movement, and thus prevents the completion of mitosis. Taxol is being used with some success as an anticancer drug.

Centrioles

Each centrosome contains a pair of centrioles.

Centrioles are built from a cylindrical array of 9 microtubules, each of which has attached to it 2 partial microtubules.

When a cell enters the cell cycle and passes through S phase, each centriole is duplicated. A "daughter" centriole grows out of the side of each parent centriole. Thus centriole replication — like DNA replication (which is occurring at the same time) — is semiconservative.

Once formed, most of the functions of the centrosomes can be accomplished without centrioles. However:

- Centrioles appear to be needed to organize the centrosome in which they are embedded.
- Sperm cells contain a pair of centrioles; eggs have none. The sperm's centrioles are absolutely essential for forming a centrosome which will form a spindle enabling the first division of the zygote to take place.
- Centrioles are also needed to make cilia and flagella.

Cilia and Flagella

Both cilia and flagella are constructed from microtubules, and both provide either:

- locomotion for the cells (e.g., sperm) or
- move fluid past the cells (e.g., ciliated epithelial cells that line our air passages and move a film of mucus towards the throat).

Both cilia and flagella have the same basic structure. If the cell has:

- many short ones, we call them cilia or
- only one or a few long ones, we call them flagella.

Each cilium (or flagellum) is made of:

- a cylindrical array of 9 evenly-spaced microtubules, each with a partial microtubule attached to it.
- 2 single microtubules run up through the center of the bundle, completing the so-called "9+2" pattern.
- The entire assembly is sheathed in a membrane that is simply an extension of the plasma membrane.

This electron micrograph (courtesy of Peter Satir) shows the 9+2 pattern of microtubules in a single cilium seen in cross section. Motion of cilia and flagella is created by the microtubules sliding past one another — Link. This requires:

- motor molecules of dynein, which link adjacent microtubules together; and
- the energy of ATP.

Each cilium or flagellum grows out from, and remains attached to, a basal body embedded in the cytoplasm. Basal bodies are identical to centrioles and are, in fact, produced by them.

Primary Cilia

Motile, "9+2", cilia are found only on certain cells in the vertebrate body, e.g., the epithelia lining the airways.

But almost every cell in vertebrates has — or had — a single primary cilium. The primary cilium grows out of the older of the two centrioles that the cell inherited following mitosis. The primary cilium does not beat because it lacks the central pair of microtubules; that is, it is "9+0". Where functions have been identified, they all involve sensory reception.

Mechanoreceptors

A primary cilium extends from the apical surface of the epithelial cells lining the kidney tubules and monitors the flow of fluid through the tubules. Inherited defects in the formation of these cilia cause polycystic kidney disease.

Chemoreceptors

We detect odors by receptors on the primary cilium of olfactory neurons.

Photoreceptors

The outer segment of the rods in the vertebrate retina is also derived from a primary cilium.

Chlorophyll

Cholorophyll is a green pigment found in most plants, algae, and cyanobacteria. Its name is derived from the Greek *chloros* "green" and *phyllon* means "leaf". Chlorophyll absorbs light most strongly in the blue and red but poorly in the green portions of the electromagnetic spectrum, hence the green colour of chlorophyll-containing tissues such as plant leaves.

Chlorophyll and Photosynthesis

Chlorophyll molecules are specifically arranged in and around pigment protein complexes called photosystems which are embedded in the thylakoid membranes of chloroplasts. In these complexes, chlorophyll serves two primary functions. The function of the vast majority of chlorophyll (up to several hundred molecules per photosystem) is to absorb light and transfer that light energy by resonance energy transfer to a specific chlorophyll pair in the reaction center of the photosystems. Because of chlorophyll's selectivity regarding the wavelength of light it absorbs, areas of a leaf containing the molecule will appear green.

The two currently accepted photosystem units are Photosystem II and Photosystem I, which have their own distinct reaction center chlorophylls, named P680 and P700, respectively. These pigments are named after the wavelength (in nanometers) of their red-peak absorption maximum. The identity, function and spectral properties of the types of chlorophyll in each photosystem are distinct and determined by each other and the protein structure surrounding them. Once extracted from the protein into a solvent (such as acetone or methanol), these chlorophyll pigments can be separated in a simple paper chromatography experiment, and, based on the number of polar groups between chlorophyll a and chlorophyll b, will chemically separate out on the paper.

The function of the reaction center chlorophyll is to use the energy absorbed by and transferred to it from the other chlorophyll pigments in the photosystems to undergo a charge separation, a specific redox reaction in which the chlorophyll donates an electron into a series of molecular intermediates called an electron transport chain. The charged reaction center chlorophyll (P680+) is then reduced back to its ground state by accepting an electron. In Photosystem II, the electron which reduces P680+ ultimately comes from the oxidation of water into O_2 and H+ through several intermediates. This reaction is how photosynthetic organisms like plants produce O_2 gas, and is the source for practically all the O_2 in Earth's atmosphere. Photosystem I typically works in series with Photosystem II, thus the P700+ of Photosystem I is usually reduced, via many intermediates in the thylakoid membrane, by electrons ultimately from Photosystem II. Electron transfer reactions in the thylakoid membranes are complex, however, and the source of electrons used to reduce P700+ can vary.

The electron flow produced by the reaction center chlorophyll pigments is used to shuttle H+ ions across the thylakoid membrane, setting up a chemiosmotic potential mainly used to produce ATP chemical energy, and those electrons ultimately reduce NADP+ to NADPH a universal reductant used to reduce CO_2 into sugars as well as for other biosynthetic reductions.

Reaction center chlorophyll-protein complexes are capable of directly absorbing light and performing charge separation events without other chlorophyll pigments, but the absorption cross section (the likelihood of absorbing a photon under a given light intensity) is small. Thus, the remaining chlorophylls in the photosystem and antenna pigment protein complexes associated with the photosystems all cooperatively absorb and funnel light energy to the reaction center. Besides chlorophyll *a*, there are other pigments, called accessory pigments, which occur in these pigment-protein antenna complexes.

Chemical Structure

Chlorophyll is a chlorin pigment, which is structurally similar to and produced through the same metabolic pathway as other porphyrin pigments such as heme. At the center of the chlorin ring is a magnesium ion. The chlorin ring can have several different side chains, usually including a long phytol chain. There are a few different forms that occur naturally, but the most widely distributed form in terrestrial plants is chlorophyll a. The general structure of chlorophyll a was elucidated by Hans Fischer in 1940, and by 1960, when most of the stereochemistry of chlorophyll a was known, Robert Burns Woodward published a total synthesis of the molecule as then known.

Spectrophotometry

Measurement of the absorption of light is complicated by the solvent used to extract it from plant material, which affects the values obtained.

- In diethyl ether, chlorophyll *a* has approximate absorbance maxima of 430 nm and 662 nm, while chlorophyll *b* has approximate maxima of 453 nm and 642 nm.

- The absorption peaks of chlorophyll *a* are at 665 nm and 465 nm. Chlorophyll *a* fluoresces at 673 nm (maximum) and 726 nm. The peak molar absorption coefficient of chlorophyll *a* exceeds 105 M-1 cm-1, which is among the highest for organic compounds.

Biosynthesis

In plants, chlorophyll may be synthesized from succinyl-CoA and glycine, although the immediate precursor to chlorophyll *a* and *b* is protochlorophyllide. In Angiosperms, the last step, conversion of protochlorophyllide to chlorophyll, is light-dependent and such plants are pale (etiolated) if grown in the darkness. Non-vascular plants and green algae have an additional light-independent enzyme and grow green in the darkness as well.

Chlorophyll itself is bound to proteins and can transfer the absorbed energy in the required direction. Protochlorophyllide, differently, mostly occur in the free form and under light conditions act as photosensitizer, forming highly toxic free radicals. Hence plants need an efficient mechanism of regulating the amount of chlorophyll precursor. In angiosperms, this is done at the step of aminolevulinic acid (ALA), one of the intermediate compounds in the biosynthesis pathway. Plants that are fed by ALA accumulate high and toxic levels of protochlorophyllide, so do the mutants with the damaged regulatory system.

Chlorosis is a condition in which leaves produce insufficient chlorophyll, turning them yellow. Chlorosis can be caused by a nutrient deficiency including iron - called iron chlorosis, or in a shortage of magnesium or nitrogen. Soil pH sometimes play a role in nutrient-caused chlorosis, many plants are adapted to grow in soils with specific pH's and their ability to absorb nutrients from the soil can be dependent on the soil pH. Chlorosis can also be caused by pathogens including viruses, bacteria and fungal infections or sap sucking insects.

Culinary Use

Chefs use chlorophyll to colour a variety of foods and beverages green, such as pasta and absinthe Chlorophyll is not soluble in water and is first mixed with a small quantity of oil to obtain the desired result.

PIGMENTS

Pigments are chemical compounds which reflect only certain wavelengths of visible light. This makes them appear "colorful". Flowers, corals, and even animal skin contain pigments which give them their colors. More important than their reflection of light is the ability of pigments to absorb certain wavelengths.

Because they interact with light to absorb only certain wavelengths, pigments are useful to plants and other autotrophs —organisms which make their own food using photosynthesis. In plants, algae, and cyanobacteria, pigments are the means by which the energy of sunlight is captured for photosynthesis. However, since each pigment reacts with only a narrow range of the spectrum, there is usually a need to produce several kinds of pigments, each of a different color, to capture more of the sun's energy.

There are three basic classes of pigments.

Chlorophylls are greenish pigments which contain a porphyrin ring. This is a stable ring-shaped molecule around which electrons are free to migrate. Because the electrons move freely, the ring has the potential to gain or lose electrons easily, and thus the potential to provide energized electrons to other molecules. This is the fundamental process by which chlorophyll "captures" the energy of sunlight.

There are several kinds of chlorophyll, the most important being chlorophyll "a". This is the molecule which makes photosynthesis possible, by passing its energized electrons on to molecules which will manufacture sugars. All plants, algae, and cyanobacteria which photosynthesize contain chlorophyll "a". A second kind of chlorophyll is chlorophyll "b", which occurs only in "green algae" and in the plants. A third form of chlorophyll which is common is (not surprisingly) called chlorophyll "c", and is found only in the photosynthetic members of the Chromista as well as the dinoflagellates. The differences between the chlorophylls of these major groups was one of the first clues that they were not as closely related as previously thought.

Carotenoids are usually red, orange, or yellow pigments, and include the familiar compound carotene, which gives carrots their color. These compounds are composed of two small six-carbon rings connected by a "chain" of carbon atoms. As a result, they do not dissolve in water, and must be attached to membranes within the cell. Carotenoids cannot transfer sunlight energy directly to the photosynthetic pathway, but must pass their absorbed energy to chlorophyll. For this reason, they are called accessory pigments. One very visible accessory pigment is fucoxanthin the brown pigment which colors kelps and other brown algae as well as the diatoms.

Phycobilins are water-soluble pigments, and are therefore found in the cytoplasm, or in the stroma of the chloroplast. They occur only in Cyanobacteria and Rhodophyta.

Phycobilins are not only useful to the organisms which use them for soaking up light energy; they have also found use as research tools. Both pycocyanin and phycoerythrin fluoresce at a particular wavelength. That is, when they are exposed to strong light, they absorb the light energy, and release it by emitting light of a very narrow range of wavelengths. The light produced by this fluorescence is so distinctive and reliable, that phycobilins may be used as chemical "tags". The pigments are chemically bonded to antibodies, which are then put into a solution of cells. When the solution is sprayed as a stream of fine droplets past a laser and computer sensor, a machine can identify whether the cells in the droplets have been "tagged" by the antibodies. This has found extensive use in cancer research, for "tagging" tumor cells.

CHAPTER

9

Photosynthesis

Photosynthesis is the process by which plants, some bacteria, and some protistans use the energy from sunlight to produce sugar, which cellular respiration converts into ATP, the "fuel" used by all living things. The conversion of unusable sunlight energy into usable chemical energy, is associated with the actions of the green pigment chlorophyll. Most of the time, the photosynthetic process uses water and releases the oxygen that we absolutely must have to stay alive. Oh yes, we need the food as well!

We can write the overall reaction of this process as:

$$6H_2O + 6CO_2 \rightarrow C_6H_{12}O_6 + 6O_2$$

Most of us don't speak chemicals, so the above chemical equation translates as:

six molecules of water plus six molecules of carbon dioxide produce one molecule of sugar plus six molecules of oxygen

Leaves and Leaf Structure

Plants are the only photosynthetic organisms to have leaves (and not all plants have leaves). A leaf may be viewed as a solar collector crammed full of photosynthetic cells.

The raw materials of photosynthesis, water and carbon dioxide, enter the cells of the leaf, and the products of photosynthesis, sugar and oxygen, leave the leaf.

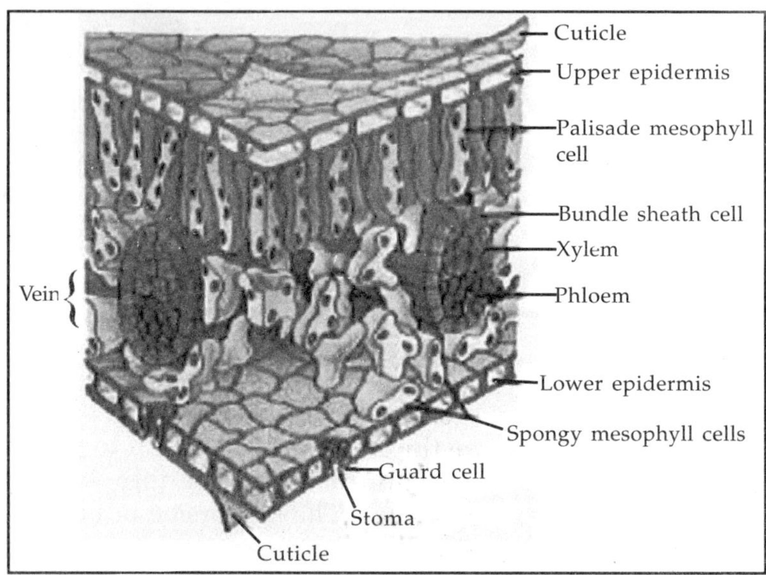

Fig. 9.1: **Cross section of a leaf, showing the anatomical features important to the study of photosynthesis: stoma, guard cell, mesophyll cells, and vein**

Water enters the root and is transported up to the leaves through specialized plant cells known as xylem (pronounces zigh-lem). Land plants must guard against drying out (desiccation) and so have evolved specialized structures known as stomata to allow gas to enter and leave the leaf. Carbon dioxide cannot pass through the protective waxy layer covering the leaf (cuticle), but it can enter the leaf through an opening (the stoma; plural = stomata; Greek for hole) flanked by two guard cells. Likewise, oxygen produced during photosynthesis can only pass out of the leaf through the opened stomata. Unfortunately for the plant, while these gases are moving between the inside and outside of the leaf, a great deal water is also lost.

Cottonwood trees, for example, will lose 100 gallons of water per hour during hot desert days. Carbon dioxide enters single-celled and aquatic autotrophs through no specialized structures.

The Nature of Light

White light is separated into the different colors (=wavelengths) of light by passing it through a prism. Wavelength is defined as the distance from peak to peak (or trough to trough). The energy of is inversely proportional to the wavelength: longer wavelengths have less energy than do shorter ones.

The order of colours is determined by the wavelength of light. Visible light is one small part of the electromagnetic spectrum. The longer the wavelength of visible light, the more red the color. Likewise the shorter wavelengths are towards the violet side of the spectrum. Wavelengths longer than red are referred to as infrared, while those shorter than violet are ultraviolet.

Light behaves both as a wave and a particle. Wave properties of light include the bending of the wave path when passing from one material (medium) into another (i.e. the prism, rainbows, pencil in a glass-of-water, etc.). The particle properties are demonstrated by the photoelectric effect. Zinc exposed to ultraviolet light becomes positively charged because light energy forces electrons from the zinc. These electrons can create an electrical current. Sodium, potassium and selenium have critical wavelengths in the visible light range. The critical wavelength is the maximum wavelength of light (visible or invisible) that creates a photoelectric effect.

Chlorophyll and Accessory Pigments

A pigment is any substance that absorbs light. The color of the pigment comes from the wavelengths of light reflected (in other words, those not absorbed). Chlorophyll, the green pigment common to all photosynthetic cells, absorbs all wavelengths of visible light except green, which it reflects to be detected by our eyes. Black pigments absorb all of the wavelengths that strike them. White pigments/ lighter colors reflect all or almost all of the energy striking them. Pigments have their own characteristic absorption spectra, the absorption pattern of a given pigment.

Chlorophyll is a complex molecule. Several modifications of chlorophyll occur among plants and other photosynthetic organisms. All photosynthetic organisms (plants, certain protistans, prochlorobacteria, and cyanobacteria) have chlorophyll a. Accessory pigments absorb energy that chlorophyll a does not absorb. Accessory pigments include chlorophyll b (also c, d, and e in algae and protistans), xanthophylls, and carotenoids (such as beta-carotene). Chlorophyll a absorbs its energy from the Violet-Blue and Reddish orange-Red wavelengths, and little from the intermediate (Green-Yellow-Orange) wavelengths.

Carotenoids and chlorophyll b absorb some of the energy in the green wavelength. Why not so much in the orange and yellow wavelengths? Both chlorophylls also absorb in the orange-red end of the spectrum (with longer wavelengths and lower energy). The origins of photosynthetic organisms in the sea may account for this. Shorter wavelengths (with more energy) do not penetrate much below 5 meters deep in sea water. The ability to absorb some energy from the longer (hence more penetrating) wavelengths might have been an advantage to early photosynthetic algae that were not able to be in the upper (photic) zone of the sea all the time.

The action spectrum of photosynthesis is the relative effectiveness of different wavelengths of light at generating electrons. If a pigment absorbs light energy, one of three things will occur. Energy is dissipated as heat. The energy may be emitted immediately as a longer wavelength, a phenomenon known as fluorescence. Energy may trigger a chemical reaction, as in photosynthesis. Chlorophyll only triggers a chemical reaction when it is associated with proteins embedded in a membrane (as in a chloroplast) or the membrane infolding found in photosynthetic prokaryotes such as cyanobacteria and prochlorobacteria.

The Structure of the Chloroplast and Photosynthetic Membranes

The *thylakoid* is the structural unit of photosynthesis. Both photosynthetic prokaryotes and eukaryotes have these flattened sacs/vesicles containing photosynthetic chemicals. Only eukaryotes have chloroplasts with a surrounding membrane.

Thylakoids are stacked like pancakes in stacks known collectively as grana. The areas between grana are referred to as stroma. While the mitochondrion has two membrane systems, the chloroplast has three, forming three compartments.

Stages of Photosynthesis

Photosynthesis is a two stage process. The first process is the Light Dependent Process (Light Reactions), requires the direct energy of light to make energy carrier molecules that are used in the second process. The Light Independent Process (or Dark Reactions) occurs when the products of the Light Reaction are used to form C-C covalent bonds of carbohydrates. The Dark Reactions can usually occur in the dark, if the energy carriers from the light process are present. Recent evidence suggests that a major enzyme of the Dark Reaction is indirectly stimulated by light, thus the term Dark Reaction is somewhat of a misnomer. The Light Reactions occur in the grana and the Dark Reactions take place in the stroma of the chloroplasts.

Light Reactions

In the Light Dependent Processes (Light Reactions) light strikes chlorophyll a in such a way as to excite electrons to a higher energy state. In a series of reactions the energy is converted (along an electron transport process) into ATP and NADPH. Water is split in the process, releasing oxygen as a by-product of the reaction. The ATP and NADPH are used to make C-C bonds in the Light Independent Process (Dark Reactions).

In the Light Independent Process, carbon dioxide from the atmosphere (or water for aquatic/marine organisms) is captured and modified by the addition of Hydrogen to form carbohydrates (general formula of carbohydrates is $[CH_2O]_n$). The incorporation of carbon dioxide into organic compounds is known as carbon fixation. The energy for this comes from the first phase of the photosynthetic process. Living systems cannot directly utilize light energy, but can, through a complicated series of reactions, convert it into C-C bond energy that can be released by glycolysis and other metabolic processes.

Photosystems are arrangements of chlorophyll and other pigments packed into thylakoids. Many Prokaryotes have only one photosystem, Photosystem II (so numbered because, while it was most likely the first to evolve, it was the second one discovered). Eukaryotes have Photosystem II plus Photosystem I. Photosystem I uses chlorophyll a, in the form referred to as P700. Photosystem II uses a form of chlorophyll a known as P680. Both "active" forms of chlorophyll a function in photosynthesis due to their association with proteins in the thylakoid membrane.

Photophosphorylation is the process of converting energy from a light-excited electron into the pyrophosphate bond of an ADP molecule. This occurs when the electrons from water are excited by the light in the presence of P680. The energy transfer is similar to the chemiosmotic electron transport occurring in the mitochondria. Light energy causes the removal of an electron from a molecule of P680 that is part of Photosystem II. The P680 requires an electron, which is taken from a water molecule, breaking the water into H+ ions and O^{-2} ions. These O^{-2} ions combine to form the diatomic O_2 that is released. The electron is "boosted" to a higher energy state and attached to a primary electron acceptor, which begins a series of redox reactions, passing the electron through a series of electron carriers, eventually attaching it to a molecule in Photosystem I. Light acts on a molecule of P700 in Photosystem I, causing an electron to be "boosted" to a still higher potential. The electron is attached to a different primary electron acceptor (that is a different molecule from the one associated with Photosystem II). The electron is passed again through a series of redox reactions, eventually being attached to $NADP^+$ and H^+ to form NADPH, an energy carrier needed in the Light Independent Reaction. The electron from Photosystem II replaces the excited electron in the P700 molecule. There is thus a continuous flow of electrons from water to NADPH. This energy is used in Carbon Fixation. Cyclic Electron Flow occurs in some eukaryotes and primitive photosynthetic bacteria. No NADPH is produced, only ATP. This occurs when cells may require additional ATP, or when there is no $NADP^+$ to reduce to NADPH. In Photosystem II, the pumping to H ions into the thylakoid and the conversion of ADP + P into ATP is driven by electron gradients established in the thylakoid membrane.

Halobacteria, which grow in extremely salty water, are facultative aerobes, they can grow when oxygen is absent. Purple pigments, known as retinal (a pigment also found in the human eye) act similar to chlorophyll. The complex of retinal and membrane proteins is known as bacteriorhodopsin, which generates electrons which establish a proton gradient that powers an ADP-ATP pump, generating ATP from sunlight without chlorophyll. This supports the theory that chemiosmotic processes are universal in their ability to generate ATP.

Dark Reaction

Dark Reaction Carbon-Fixing Reactions are also known as the Dark Reactions (or Light Independent Reactions). Carbon dioxide enters single-celled and aquatic autotrophs through no specialized structures, diffusing into the cells. Land plants must guard against drying out (desiccation) and so have evolved specialized structures known as stomata to allow gas to enter and leave the leaf. The Calvin Cycle occurs in the stroma of chloroplasts (where would it occur in a prokaryote?). Carbon dioxide is captured by the chemical ribulose biphosphate (RuBP). RuBP is a 5-C chemical. Six molecules of carbon dioxide enter the Calvin Cycle, eventually producing one molecule of glucose.

The first stable product of the Calvin Cycle is phosphoglycerate (PGA), a 3-C chemical. The energy from ATP and NADPH energy carriers generated by the photosystems is used to attach phosphates to (phosphorylate) the PGA. Eventually there are 12 molecules of glyceraldehyde phosphate (also known as phosphoglyceraldehyde or PGAL, a 3-C), two of which are removed from the cycle to make a glucose. The remaining PGAL molecules are converted by ATP energy to reform 6 RuBP molecules, and thus start the cycle again. Remember the complexity of life, each reaction in this process, as in Kreb's Cycle, is catalyzed by a different reaction-specific enzyme.

C-4 Pathway

Some plants have developed a preliminary step to the Calvin Cycle (which is also referred to as a C-3 pathway), this preamble step is known as C-4. While most C-fixation begins with RuBP, C-4 begins with a new molecule, phosphoenolpyruvate (PEP), a 3-C chemical that is converted into oxaloacetic acid (OAA, a 4-C chemical) when carbon dioxide is combined with PEP. The OAA is converted to Malic Acid and then transported from the mesophyll cell into the bundle-sheath cell, where OAA is broken down into

PEP plus carbon dioxide. The carbon dioxide then enters the Calvin Cycle, with PEP returning to the mesophyll cell. The resulting sugars are now adjacent to the leaf veins and can readily be transported throughout the plant.

The capture of carbon dioxide by PEP is mediated by the enzyme PEP carboxylase, which has a stronger affinity for carbon dioxide than does RuBP carboxylase When carbon dioxide levels decline below the threshold for RuBP carboxylase, RuBP is catalyzed with oxygen instead of carbon dioxide. The product of that reaction forms glycolic acid, a chemical that can be broken down by photorespiration, producing neither NADH nor ATP, in effect dismantling the Calvin Cycle. C-4 plants, which often grow close together, have had to adjust to decreased levels of carbon dioxide by artificially raising the carbon dioxide concentration in certain cells to prevent photorespiration. C-4 plants evolved in the tropics and are adapted to higher temperatures than are the C-3 plants found at higher latitudes. Common C-4 plants include crabgrass, corn, and sugar cane. Note that OAA and Malic Acid also have functions in other processes, thus the chemicals would have been present in all plants, leading scientists to hypothesize that C-4 mechanisms evolved several times independently in response to a similar environmental condition, a type of evolution known as convergent evolution.

The Carbon Cycle

Plants may be viewed as carbon sinks, removing carbon dioxide from the atmosphere and oceans by fixing it into organic chemicals. Plants also produce some carbon dioxide by their respiration, but this is quickly used by photosynthesis. Plants also convert energy from light into chemical energy of C-C covalent bonds. Animals are carbon dioxide producers that derive their energy from carbohydrates and other chemicals produced by plants by the process of photosynthesis.

The balance between the plant carbon dioxide removal and animal carbon dioxide generation is equalized also by the formation of carbonates in the oceans. This removes excess carbon dioxide from the air and water (both of which are in equilibrium with regard to carbon dioxide). Fossil fuels, such as petroleum and coal, as well as more recent fuels such as peat and wood generate carbon dioxide when burned. Fossil fuels are formed ultimately by organic processes, and represent also a tremendous carbon sink. Human activity has greatly increased the concentration of carbon dioxide in air. This increase has led to global warming, an increase in temperatures around the world, the Greenhouse Effect. The increase in carbon dioxide and other pollutants in the air has also led to acid rain, where water falls through polluted air and chemically combines with carbon dioxide, nitrous oxides, and sulfur oxides, producing rainfall with pH as low as 4. This results in fish kills and changes in soil pH which can alter the natural vegetation and uses of the land. The Global Warming problem can lead to melting of the ice caps in Greenland and Antarctica, raising sea-level as much as 120 meters. Changes in sea-level and temperature would affect climate changes, altering belts of grain production and rainfall patterns.

Porphyrin

Porphyrins are a group of chemical compounds of which many occur in nature, such as in green leaves and red blood cells, and in bio-inspired synthetic catalysts and devices. They are heterocyclic macrocycles characterised by the presence of one pyrroline and three pyrrole chemical groups interconnected via their a carbon atoms via methine bridges (=CH-). Porphyrins are aromatic, and they obey Hückel's rule for aromaticity in that they possess 4n+2 pi π electrons that are delocalized over the macrocycle. The macrocycle, therefore, is a highly-conjugated system, and, as a consequence, is deeply colored - the name porphyrin comes from a Greek word for *purple*. The macrocycle has 26 pi electrons. The parent porphyrin is porphine, and substituted porphines are called porphyrins.

Complexes of Porphyrins and Related Molecules

Porphyrins bind metals to form complexes. The metal ion, usually with a charge of 2+ or 3+, is in the central N_4 cavity formed by the loss of two protons. Most metals can be inserted. A schematic equation for these syntheses is shown:

H_2porphyrin + $[ML_n]^{2+} \rightarrow$ M(porphyrinate)L_{n-4} + 4 L + 2 H^+

A porphyrin in which no metal is inserted in its cavity is sometimes called a *free base*. Some iron-containing porphyrins are called hemes; and heme-containing proteins, or *hemoproteins*, are found extensively in nature. Hemoglobin and myoglobin are two O_2-binding proteins that contain iron porphyrins.

Related to porphyrins are several other heterocycles, including corrins, chlorins, bacteriochlorophylls, and corphins. Chlorins (2, 3-dihydroporphyrin) are more reduced, contain more hydrogen than porphyrins, and feature a pyrroline subunit. This structure occurs in chlorophyll. Replacement of two of the four pyrrolic subunits with pyrrolinic subunits results in either a bacteriochlorin (as found in some photosynthetic bacteria) or an isobacteriochlorin, depending on the relative positions of the reduced rings. Some porphyrin derivatives follow Hückel's rule, but most do not.

Laboratory Synthesis

One of the more common syntheses for porphyrins is based on work by Paul Rothemund His techniques underpin more modern syntheses such as those described by Adler and Longo The synthesis of simple porphyrins such as *meso*-tetraphenylporphyrin (H_2TPP) is also commonly done in university teaching labs.

In this method, porphyrins are assembled from pyrrole and substituted aldehydes. Acidic conditions are essential; formic acid, acetic acid, and propionic acid are typical reaction solvents, or p-toluenesulfonic acid can be used with a non-acidic solvent. Lewis acids such as boron trifluoride etherate and ytterbium triflate have also been known to catalyse porphyrin formation. A large amount of side-product is formed and is removed, usually by chromatography.

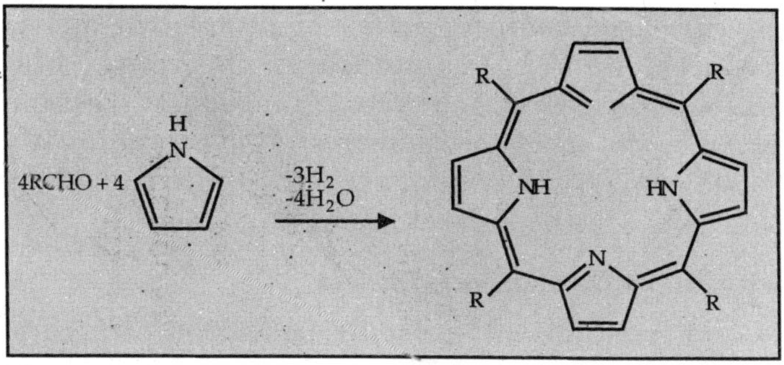

4RCHO + 4 (pyrrole) $\xrightarrow[-4H_2O]{-3H_2}$ (porphyrin)

Fig. 10.1

Biosynthesis

The "committed step" for porphyrin biosynthesis is the formation of D-aminolevulinic acid (dALA) by the reaction of the amino acid glycine and succinyl-CoA, from the citric acid cycle. Two molecules of dALA combine to give porphobilinogen (PBG), which contains a pyrrole ring. Four PBGs are then combined through deamination into hydroxymethyl bilane (HMB), which is hydrolysed to form the circular tetrapyrrole uroporphyrinogen III. This molecule undergoes a number of further modifications. Intermediates are used in different species to form particular substances, but, in humans, the main end-product protoporphyrin IX is combined with iron to form heme. Bile pigments are the breakdown products of heme.

The following scheme summarizes the biosynthesis of porphyrins, with references by EC number and the OMIM database. The porphyria associated with the deficiency of each enzyme is also shown.

Applications

Although natural porphyrin complexes are essential for life, synthetic porphyrins and their complexes have limited utility. Complexes of meso-tetraphenylporphyrin, e.g., the iron-(III) chloride complex (TPPFeCl) catalyse a variety of reactions in organic chemistry, but none is of practical value.

Porphyrin-based compounds are of interest in molecular electronics and supramolecular building blocks. Phthalocyanines, which are structurally related to porphyrins, are used in commerce as dyes and catalysts. Synthetic porphyrin dyes that are incorporated in the design of solar cells are the subject of ongoing research.

Supramolecular Chemistry

Porphyrins are often used to construct structures in supramolecular chemistry. These systems take advantage of the Lewis acidity of the metal, typically zinc. An example of a host-guest complex that was constructed from a macrocycle composed of four porphyrins A guest-free base porphyrin is bound to the center by coordination with its four pyridine sustituents.

PORPHYRIA

Porphyrias are a group of inherited or acquired disorders of certain enzymes in the heme biosynthetic pathway (also called porphyrin pathway). They are broadly classified as acute (hepatic) porphyrias and cutaneous (erythropoietic) porphyrias, based on the site of the overproduction and accumulation of the porphyrins (or their chemical precursors). They manifest with either skin problems or with neurological complications (or occasionally both). A clinically and histologically identical condition is called pseudoporphyria. Pseudoporphyria is characterized by normal serum and urine porphyrin levels.

The term derives from the Greek p , *porphyra,* meaning "purple pigment". The name is likely to have been a reference to the purple discolouration of feces and urine in patients during an attack. Although original descriptions are attributed to Hippocrates, the disease was first explained biochemically by Dr Felix Hoppe-Seyler in 1874, and acute porphyrias were described by the Dutch physician Prof. B.J. Stokvis in 1889.

Signs and Symptoms

Acute Porphyria

The acute, or hepatic, porphyrias primarily affect the nervous system, resulting in abdominal pain, vomiting, acute neuropathy, seizures and mental disturbances, including hallucinations, depression, anxiety and paranoia. Cardiac arrhythmias and tachycardia (fast heart rate) may develop as the autonomic nervous system is affected. Pain can be severe and can, in some cases, be both acute and chronic in nature. Constipation is frequently present, as the nervous system of the gut is affected, but diarrhea can also occur.

Given the many presentations and the relatively uncommon occurrence of porphyria the patient may initially be suspected to have other, unrelated conditions. For instance, the polyneuropathy of acute porphyria may be mistaken for Guillain-Barré syndrome, and porphyria testing is commonly recommended in those scenarios Systemic lupus erythematosus features photosensitivity, pain attacks and shares various other symptoms with porphyria.

Not all porphyrias are genetic, and patients with liver disease who develop porphyria as a result of liver dysfunction may exhibit other signs of their condition, such as jaundice.

Patients with acute porphyria (PCT, AIP, HCP, VP) are at increased risk over their life for hepatocellular carcinoma (primary liver cancer) and may require monitoring. Other typical risk factors for liver cancer need not be present, such as hepatitis B or C, iron overload or alcoholic cirrhosis.

Cutaneous Porphyria

The cutaneous, or erythropoietic, porphyrias primarily affect the skin, causing photosensitivity (photodermatitis), blisters, necrosis of the skin and gums, itching, and swelling, and increased hair growth on areas such as the forehead. Often there is no abdominal pain, distinguishing it from other porphyrias.

In some forms of porphyria, accumulated heme precursors excreted in the urine may cause various changes in color, after exposure to sunlight, to a dark reddish or dark brown color. Even a purple hue or red urine may be seen. Heme precursors may also accumulate in the teeth and fingernails, giving them a reddish appearance.

Diagnosis

Porphyrin Studies

Porphyria is diagnosed through spectroscopy and biochemical analysis of blood, urine, and stool. In general, urine estimation of porphobilinogen (PBG) is the first step if acute porphyria is suspected. As a result of feedback, the decreased production of heme leads to increased production of precursors, PBG being one of the first substances in the porphyrin synthesis pathway In nearly all cases of acute porphyria syndromes, urinary PBG is markedly elevated except for the very rare ALA dehydratase deficiency or in patients with symptoms due to hereditary tyrosinemia type I In cases of mercury- or arsenic poisoning-induced porphyria, other changes in porphyrin profiles appear, most notably elevations of uroporphyrins I&III, coproporphyrins I & III and pre-coproporphyrin.

Repeat testing during an attack and subsequent attacks may be necessary in order to detect a porphyria, as levels may be normal or near-normal between attacks. The urine screening test has been known to fail in the initial stages of a severe life threatening attack of acute intermittent porphyria.

The bulk (up to 90%) of the genetic carriers of the more common, dominantly inherited acute hepatic porphyrias (acute intermittent porphyria, hereditary coproporphyria, variegate porphyria) have been noted in DNA tests to be latent for classic symptoms and may require DNA or enzyme testing. The exception to this may be latent post-puberty genetic carriers of hereditary coproporphyria.

As most porphyrias are rare conditions, general hospital labs typically do not have the expertise, technology or staff time to perform porphyria testing. In general, testing involves sending samples of blood, stool and urine to a reference laboratory. All samples to detect porphyrins must be handled properly. Samples should be taken during an acute attack, otherwise a false negative result may occur. Samples must be protected from light and either refrigerated or preserved.

If all the porphyrin studies are negative, one has to consider pseudoporphyria. A careful medication review often will find the inciting cause of pseudoporphyria.

Additional Tests

Further diagnostic tests of affected organs may be required, such as nerve conduction studies for neuropathy or an ultrasound of the liver. Basic biochemical tests may assist in identifying liver disease, hepatocellular carcinoma, and other organ problems.

Pathogenesis

In humans, porphyrins are the main precursors of heme, an essential constituent of hemoglobin, myoglobin, catalase, peroxidase, respiratory and P450 liver cytochromes.

Deficiency in the enzymes of the porphyrin pathway leads to insufficient production of heme. Heme function plays a central role in cellular metabolism. This is not the main problem in the porphyrias; most heme synthesis enzymes—even dysfunctional enzymes—have enough residual activity to assist in heme biosynthesis. The principal problem in these deficiencies is the accumulation of porphyrins, the heme precursors, which are toxic to tissue in high concentrations. The chemical properties of these intermediates determine the location of accumulation, whether they induce photosensitivity, and whether the intermediate is excreted (in the urine or feces).

There are eight enzymes in the heme biosynthetic pathway, four of which—the first one and the last three—are in the mitochondria, while the other four are in the cytosol. Defects in any of these can lead to some form of porphyria.

The hepatic porphyrias are characterized by acute neurological attacks (seizures, psychosis, extreme back and abdominal pain and an acute polyneuropathy), while the erythropoietic forms present with skin problems, usually a light-sensitive blistering rash and increased hair growth.

Variegate porphyria (also *porphyria variegata* or *mixed porphyria*), which results from a partial deficiency in PROTO oxidase, manifests itself with skin lesions similar to those of porphyria cutanea tarda combined with acute neurologic attacks. All other porphyrias are either skin-or nerve-predominant.

Plant Defense Against Herbivory

Plant defense against herbivory or host-plant resistance (HPR) includes a range of adaptations evolved by plants that improve their survival and reproduction by reducing the impact of herbivores.

There are four basic strategies plants use to reduce damage by herbivores. One strategy is to escape or avoid herbivores in time or in place, for example by growing in a location where plants are not easily found or accessed by herbivores or by repelling herbivores chemically (also termed non-preference or antixenosis). Another approach is the plant tolerates herbivores, by diverting the herbivore to eat non-essential parts of the plant, or developing an enhanced ability to recover from the damage caused by herbivory. Some plants encourage the presence of natural enemies of herbivores, which in turn protect the plant from herbivores. Finally, plants protect themselves by confrontation; the use of chemical or mechanical defenses, such as toxins that kill herbivores or reduce plant digestibility (also called antibiosis) These defenses can either be *constitutive*, always present in the plant, or *induced*, produced in reaction to damage or stress caused by herbivores.

Historically, insects have been the most significant herbivores, and the evolution of land plants is closely associated with the evolution of insects. While most plant defenses are directed against insects, other defenses have evolved that are aimed at vertebrate herbivores, such as birds and mammals. The study of plant defenses against herbivory is important, not only from an evolutionary view point, but also in the direct impact that these defenses have on agriculture, including human and livestock food sources, as well as the in the search for plants of medical importance.

Plant Evolution

The earliest land plants evolved from aquatic plants around 450 million years ago (Ma) in the Ordovician period. These early land plants had no vascular system and required free water for their reproduction. Vascular plants appeared later and their diversification began in the Devonian era (about 400 Ma). Their reduced dependence on water resulted from adaptations such as protective coatings to reduce evaporation from their tissues. Reproduction and dispersal of vascular plants in these dry conditions was achieved through the evolution of specialized seed structures. The diversification of flowering plants (angiosperms) during the Cretaceous period is associated with the sudden burst of speciation in insects. This diversification of insects represented a major selective force in plant evolution, and led to selection of plants that had defensive adaptations. Early insect herbivores were mandibulate and bit or chewed vegetation; but the evolution of vascular plants lead to the co-evolution of other forms of herbivory, such as sap-sucking, leaf mining, gall forming and nectar-feeding.

Records of Herbivory

Our understanding of herbivory in geological time comes from three sources: fossilised plants, which may preserve evidence of defence (such as spines), or herbivory-related damage; the observation of plant debris in fossilised animal faeces; and the construction of herbivore mouthparts.

Long thought to be a Mesozoic phenomenon, evidence for herbivory is found almost as soon as fossils which could show it. Within under 20 million years of the first fossils of sporangia and stems towards the close of the Silurian, around 420 million years ago, there is evidence that they were being consumed. Animals fed on the spores of early Devonian plants, and the Rhynie chert also provides evidence that organisms fed on plants using a "pierce and suck" technique. Many plants of this time are preserved with spine-like enations, which may have performed a defensive role before being co-opted to develop into leaves.

During the ensuing 75 million years, plants evolved a range of more complex organs - from roots to seeds. There was a gap of 50 to 100 million years between each organ evolving, and it being fed upon Hole feeding and skeletonisation are recorded in the early Permian, with surface fluid feeding evolving by the end of that period.

Co-evolution

Herbivores depend on plants for food, and have evolved mechanisms to obtain this food despite the evolution of a diverse arsenal of plant defenses. Herbivore adaptations to plant defense have been likened to *offensive traits* and consist of adaptations that allow increased feeding and use of a host plant Relationships between herbivores and their host plants often results in reciprocal evolutionary change, called co-evolution. When an herbivore eats a plant it selects for plants that can mount a defensive response. In cases where this relationship demonstrates *specificity* (the evolution of each trait is due to the other), and *reciprocity* (both traits must evolve), the species are thought to have co-evolved. The "escape and radiation" mechanism for co-evolution presents the idea that adaptations in herbivores and their host plants have been the driving force behind speciation and have played a role in the radiation of insect species during the age of angiosperms Some herbivores have evolved ways to hijack plant defenses to their own benefit, by sequestering these chemicals and using them to protect themselves from predators.

Types

Plant defenses can be classified generally as induced or constitutive. Constitutive defenses are always present in the plant species, while induced defenses are synthesized or mobilized to the site where a plant is injured. There are wide variations in the composition and concentration of constitutive defenses and these range from mechanical defenses to digestibility reducers and toxins. Most external mechanical defenses and large quantitative defenses are constitutive, as they require large amounts of resources to produce and difficult to mobilize.

Induced defenses include secondary metabolic products, as well as morphological and physiological changes. An advantage of inducible, rather than constitutive defenses, is that increased variability increases the effectiveness of the defenses This advantage comes from the suggestion that if herbivores can choose among different plants and plant tissues, they may avoid eating plants that have both constitutive and induced defenses.

Chemical Defenses

The evolution of chemical defenses in plants is linked to the emergence of chemical substances that are not involved in the essential photosynthetic and metabolic activities. These substances, secondary metabolites, are organic compounds that are not directly involved in the normal growth, development or reproduction of organisms and often produced as by-products during the synthesis of primary metabolic products These secondary metabolites play a major role in defenses against herbivores.

Secondary metabolites are often characterized as either qualitative or quantitative. Qualitative metabolites are defined as toxins that interfere with an herbivore's metabolism, often by blocking specific biochemical reactions. Qualitative chemicals are present in plants in relatively low concentrations (often less than 2% dry weight), and are not dosage dependent. These defenses have morphological properties (i.e. water soluble, small molecules, and are energetically inexpensive) that facilitate rapid synthesis, transport, and storage. These chemicals are effective against non-adapted specialists and generalist herbivores.

Quantitative chemicals are those that are present in high concentration in plants (5-40% dry weight) and are equally effective against all specialists and generalist herbivores. Most quantitative metabolites are digestibility reducers that make plant cell walls indigestible to animals. The effects of quantitative metabolites are dosage dependent and the higher these chemicals' proportion in the herbivore's diet, the less nutrition the herbivore can gain from ingesting plant tissues. Because they are typically large molecules, these defenses are energetically expensive to produce and maintain, and often take longer than smaller, qualitative chemicals to synthesize and transport, therefore these chemicals are expected to serve an important purpose within the plant.

Types of Chemical Defenses

Plants have developed many secondary metabolites involved in plant defense, which are collectively known as anti-herbivory compounds and can be classified into three sub-groups: nitrogen compounds (including *alkaloids*, *cyanogenic glycosides* and *glucosinolates*), *terpenoids*, and *phenolics*.

Alkaloids are derived from various amino acids. Over 3000 known alkaloids exist, examples include nicotine, caffeine, morphine, colchicine, ergolines, strychnine, and quinine. Alkaloids have pharmacological effects on humans and other animals. Some alkaloids can inhibit or activate enzymes, or alter carbohydrate and fat storage by inhibiting the formation phosphodiester bonds involved in their breakdown. Certain alkaloids bind to nucleic acids and can inhibit synthesis of proteins and affect DNA repair mechanisms. Alkaloids can also affect cell membrane and cytoskeletal structure causing the cells to weaken, collapse, or leak, and can affect nerve transmission.

Cyanogenic glycosides are stored in inactive forms in plant vacuoles. They become toxic when herbivores eat the plant and break cell membranes allowing the glycosides to come into contact with enzymes in the cytoplasm releasing hydrogen cyanide which blocks cellular respiration. Glucosinolates are activated in much the same way as cyanogenic glucosides, and the products can cause gastroenteritis, salivation, diarrhea, and irritation of the mouth.

The terpenoids, sometimes referred to as isoprenoids, are organic chemicals similar to terpenes, derived from five-carbon isoprene units. There are over 10,000 known types of terpenoids Most are multicyclic structures which differ from one another in both functional groups, and in basic carbon skeletons Monoterpenoids, continuing 2 isoprene units, are volatile essential oils such as citronella, limonene, menthol, camphor, and pinene. Diterpenoids, 4 isoprene units, are widely distributed in latex and resins, and can be quite toxic. Diterpenes are responsible for making Rhododendron leaves poisonous. Plant steroids and sterols are also produced from terpenoid precursors, including vitamin D, glycosides (such as digitalis) and saponins (which lyse red blood cells of herbivores).

Phenolics, sometimes called phenols, consist of an aromatic 6-carbon ring bonded to a hydroxy group. Some phenols have antiseptic properties, while others disrupt endocrine activity. Phenolics range from simple tannins to the more complex flavonoids that give plants much of their red, blue, yellow, and white pigments. Complex phenolics called polyphenols are capable of producing many different types of effects on humans, including antioxidant properties. Some examples of phenolics used for defense in plants are: lignin, silymarin and cannabinoids Condensed tannins, polymers composed of 2 to 50 (or more) flavonoid molecules, inhibit herbivore digestion by binding to consumed plant proteins and making them more difficult for animals to digest, and by interfering with protein absorption and digestive enzymes Silica and lignins, which are completely indigestible to animals, grind down insect mandibles (appendages necessary for feeding).

In addition to the three larger groups of substances mentioned above, fatty acid derivates, amino acids and even peptides are used as defence. The cholinergic toxine, cicutoxin of water hemlock, is an polyyne derived from the fatty acid metabolism ß-N-Oxalyl-L-α, ß-diaminopropionic acid as simple amino acid is used by the sweet pea which leads also to intoxication in humans. The synthesis of fluoroacetate in several plants is an example for the use of small molecules to disturb the metabolism of the herbivore, in this case the citric acid cycle.

Mechanical Defenses

Plants have many external structural defenses that discourage herbivory. Depending on the herbivore's physical characteristics (i.e. size and defensive armor), plant structural defenses on stems and leaves can deter, injure, or kill the grazer. Some defensive compounds are produced internally but are released onto the plant's surface; for example, resins, lignins, silica, and wax cover the epidermis of terrestrial plants and alter the texture of the plant tissue. The leaves of holly plants, for instance, are very smooth and slippery making feeding difficult. Some plants produce gummosis or sap that traps insects.

A plant's leaves and stem may be covered with sharp spines or trichomes- hairs on the leaf often with barbs, sometimes containing irritants or poisons. Plant structural features like spines and thorns reduce feeding by large ungulate herbivores (e.g. kudu, impala, and goats) by restricting the herbivores' feeding rate, or by wearing down the molars as in pears The structure of a plant, its branching and leaf arrangement may also be evolved to reduce herbivore impact. The shrubs of New Zealand have evolved special wide branching adaptations believed to be a response to browsing birds such as the moas Similarly, African Acacias have dense thorns on the outside, but none in the middle of the crown, which is comparatively safe from herbivores such as giraffes. Young Acacias, which would be vulnerable due to their proximity to the ground, display a profusion of thorns gradually decreasing with age.

Trees such as coconut and other palms, may protect their fruit by multiple layers of armour, needing efficient tools to break through to the seed contents, and special skills to climb the tall and relatively smooth trunk.

Thigmonasty

Thigmonastic movements, those that occur in response to touch, are used as a defense in some plants. The leaves of the sensitive plant, *Mimosa pudica*, close up rapidly in response to direct touch, vibration, or even electrical and thermal stimuli. The proximate cause of this mechanical response is an abrupt change in the turgor pressure in the pulvini at the base of leaves resulting from osmotic phenomena. This is then spread via both electrical and chemical means through the plant; only a single leaflet need be disturbed.

This response lowers the surface area available to herbivores, which are presented with the underside of each leaflet, and results in a wilted appearance. It may also physically dislodge small herbivores, such as insects

Thigmonasty is not only useful in discouraging herbivores, however. For instance the venus flytrap makes use of it to catch its own food.

Mimicry and Camouflage

Some plants mimic the presence of insect eggs on their leaves, dissuading insect species from laying their eggs there. Because female butterflies are less likely to lay their eggs on plants that already have butterfly eggs, some species of neotropical vines of the genus *Passiflora* (Passion flowers) contain physical structures resembling the yellow eggs of *Heliconius* butterflies on their leaves, which discourage oviposition by butterflies.

Indirect Defenses

Another category of plant defenses are those features that indirectly protect the plant by enhancing the probability of attracting the natural enemies of herbivores. Such an arrangement is known as mutualism, in this case of the "enemy of my enemy" variety. One such feature are semiochemicals, given off by plants. Semiochemicals are a group of volatile organic compounds involved in interactions between organisms. One group of semiochemicals are allelochemics; consisting of allomones, which play a defensive role in interspecies communication, and kairomones, which are used by members of higher trophic levels to locate food sources. When a plant is attacked it releases allelochemics containing an abnormal ratio of volatiles Predators sense these volatiles as food cues, attracting them to the damaged plant, and to feeding herbivores. The subsequent reduction in the number of herbivores confers a fitness benefit to the plant and demonstrates the indirect defensive capabilities of semiochemicals. Induced volatiles also have drawbacks, however; some studies have suggested that these volatiles also attract herbivores.

Plants also provide housing and food items for natural enemies of herbivores, known as "biotic" defense mechanisms, as a means to maintain their presence. For example, trees from the genus *Macaranga* have adapted their thin stem walls to create ideal housing for an ant species (genus *Crematogaster*), which, in turn, protects the plant from herbivores In addition to providing housing, the plant also provides the ant with its exclusive food source; from the food bodies produced by the plant. Similarly, some *Acacia* tree species have developed thorns that are swollen at the base, forming a hollowing structure that acts as housing. Theses *Acacia* trees also produce nectar in extrafloral nectaries on their leaves as food for the ants.

Most plants have endophytes, microbial organisms that live within them. While some cause disease, others protect plants from herbivores and pathogenic microbes. Endophytes can help the plant by producing toxins harmful to other organisms that would attack the plant, such as alkaloid producing fungi which are common in grasses such as tall fescue (*Festuca arundinacea*).

Leaf Shedding and Colour

There have been suggestions that leaf shedding may be a response that provides protection against diseases and certain kinds of pests such as leaf miners and gall forming insects Other responses such as the change of leaf colours prior to fall have also been suggested as adaptations that may help undermine the camouflage of herbivores Autumn leaf color has also been suggested to act as an honest warning signal of defensive commitment towards insect pests that migrate to the trees in autumn.

Costs and Benefits

Defensive structures and chemicals are costly as they require resources that could otherwise be used by plants to maximize growth and reproduction. Many models have been proposed to explore how and why some plants make this investment in defenses against herbivores.

Optimal Defense Hypothesis

The optimal defense hypothesis attempts to explain how the kinds of defenses a particular plant might use reflect the threats each individual plant faces This model considers three main factors, namely: risk of attac.

The first factor determining optimal defense is risk: how likely is it that a plant or certain plant parts will be attacked? This is also related to the *plant apparency hypothesis*, which states that a plant will invest heavily in broadly effective defenses when the plant is easily found by herbivores. Examples of apparent plants that produce generalized protections include long-living trees, shrubs, and perennial grasses. Unapparent plants, such as short-lived plants of early successional stages, on the other hand, preferentially invest in small amounts of qualitative toxins that are effective against all but the most specialized herbivores

The second factor is the value of protection: would the plant be less able to survive and reproduce after removal of part of its structure by a herbivore? Not all plant parts are of equal evolutionary value, thus valuable parts contain more defenses. A plant's stage of development at the time of feeding also affects the resulting change in fitness. Experimentally, the fitness value of a plant structure is determined by removing that part of the plant and observing the effect. In general, reproductive parts are not as easily replaced as vegetative parts, terminal leaves have greater value than basal leaves, and the loss of plant parts mid-season has a greater negative effect on fitness than removal at the beginning or end of the season. Seeds in particular tend to be very well protected. For example, the seeds of many edible fruits and nuts contain cyanogenic glycosides such as amygdalin. This results from the need to balance the effort needed to make the fruit attractive to animal dispersers while ensuring that the seeds are not destroyed by the animal.

The final consideration is cost: how much will a particular defensive strategy cost a plant in energy and materials? This is particularly important, as energy spent on defense cannot be used for other functions, such as reproduction and growth. The optimal defense hypothesis predicts that plants will allocate more energy towards defense when the benefits of protection outweigh the costs, specifically in situations where there is high herbivore pressure.

Carbon: Nutrient Balance Hypothesis

The carbon nutrient balance hypothesis, also known as the *environmental constraint hypothesis*, states that the various types of plant defenses are responses to variations in the levels of nutrients in the environment This hypothesis predicts the Carbon/Nitrogen ratio in plants determines which secondary metabolites will be synthesized. For example, plants growing in nitrogen-poor soils will use carbon-based defenses (mostly digestibility reducers), while those growing in low-carbon environments (such as shady conditions) are more likely to produce nitrogen-based toxins. The hypothesis further predicts that plants can change their defences in response to changes in nutrients. For example, if plants are grown in low-nitrogen conditions, then these plants will implement a defensive strategy composed of constitutive carbon-based defenses. If nutrient levels subsequently increase, by for example the addition of fertilizers, these carbon-based defenses will decrease.

Growth Rate Hypothesis

The growth rate hypothesis, also known as the *resource availability hypothesis*, states that defense strategies are determined by the inherent growth rate of the plant, which is in turn determined by the resources available to the plant. A major assumption is that available resources are the limiting factor in determining the maximum growth rate of a plant species. This model predicts that the level of defense investment will increase as the potential of growth decreases Additionally, plants in resource-poor areas, with inherently slow-growth rates, tend to have long-lived leaves and twigs, and the loss of plant appendages may result in a loss of scarce and valuable nutrients.

A recent test of this model involved a reciprocal transplants of seedlings of 20 species of trees between clay soils (nutrient rich) and white sand (nutrient poor) to determine whether trade-offs between growth rate and defenses restrict species to one habitat. Seedlings originating from the nutrient-poor sand had higher levels of constitutive carbon-based defenses, but when they were transplanted into nutrient-rich clay soils, they experienced higher mortality from herbivory. These finding suggest that defensive strategies limit the habitats of some plants.

Growth-differentiation Balance Hypothesis

The growth-differentiation balance hypothesis states that plant defenses are a result of a tradeoff between "growth-related processes" and "differentiation-related processes" in different environments. Differentiation-related processes are defined as "processes that enhance the structure or function of existing cells (i.e. maturation and specialization). A plant will produce chemical defenses only when energy is available from photosynthesis and plants with the highest concentrations of secondary metabolites are the ones with an intermediate level of available resources. The GDBH also accounts for tradeoffs between growth and defense over a resource availability gradient. In situations where resources (e.g. water and nutrients) limit photosynthesis, carbon supply is predicted to limit both growth and defense. As resource availability increases, the requirements needed to support photosynthesis are met, allowing for accumulation of carbohydrate in tissues. As resources are not sufficient to meet the large demands of growth, these carbon compounds can instead be partitioned into the synthesis of carbon based secondary metabolites (phenolics, tannins, etc.). In environments where the resource demands for growth are met, carbon is allocated to rapidly dividing meristems (high sink strength) at the expense of secondary metabolism. Thus rapidly growing plants are predicted to contain lower levels of secondary metabolites and vice versa. In addition, the tradeoff predicted by the GDBH may change over time, as evidenced by a recent study on Salix spp. Much support for this hypothesis is present in the literature, and some scientists consider the GDBH the most mature of the plant defense hypotheses.

Importance to Humans

Agriculture

The variation of plant susceptibility to pests was probably known even in the early stages of agriculture in humans. In historic times, the observation of such variations in susceptibility have provided solutions for major socio-economic problems. The grape phylloxera was introduced from North America to France in 1860 and in 25 years it destroyed nearly a third (100,000 km^2) of the French grape yards. Charles Valentine Riley noted that the American species *Vitis labrusca* was resistant to *Phylloxera*. Riley, with J.E. Planchon, helped save the French wine industry by suggesting the grafting of the susceptible but high quality grapes onto *Vitis labrusca* root stocks. The formal study of plant resistance to herbivory was first covered extensively in 1951 by Reginald (R.H.) Painter, who is widely regarded as the founder of this area of research, in his book *Plant Resistance to Insects* While this work pioneered further research in the US, the work of Chesnokov was the basis of further research in the USSR.

Fresh growth of grass is sometimes high in prussic acid content and can cause poisoning of grazing livestock. The production of cyanogenic chemicals in grasses is primarily a defense against herbivores.

The human innovation of cooking may have been particularly helpful in overcoming many of the defensive chemicals of plants. Many enzyme inhibitors in cereal grains and pulses, such as trypsin inhibitors prevalent in pulse crops, are denatured by cooking, making them digestible.

It has been known since the late 17th century that plants contain noxious chemicals which are avoided by insects. These chemicals have been used by man as early insecticides; in 1690 nicotine was extracted from tobacco and used as a contact insecticide. In 1773, insect infested plants were treated with nicotine fumigation by heating tobacco and blowing the smoke over the plants. The flowers of *Chrysanthemum* species contain pyrethrin which is a potent insecticide. In later years, the applications of plant resistance became an important area of research in agriculture and plant breeding, particularly because they can serve as a safe and low-cost alternative to the use of pesticides The important role of secondary plant substances in plant defense was described in the late 1950s by Vincent Dethier and G.S. Fraenkel The use of botanical pesticides is widespread and notable examples include Azadirachtin from the neem (*Azadirachta indica*), d-Limonene from Citrus species, Rotenone from *Derris*, Capsaicin from Chili Pepper and Pyrethrum.

The selective breeding of crop plants often involves selection against the plant's intrinsic resistance strategies. This makes crop plant varieties particularly susceptible to pests unlike their wild relatives. In breeding for host-plant resistance, it is often the wild relatives that provide the source of resistance genes. These genes are incorporated using conventional approaches to plant breeding, but have also been augmented by recombinant techniques, which allow introduction of genes from completely unrelated organisms. The most famous transgenic approach is the introduction of genes from the bacterial species, *Bacillus thuringiensis*, into plants. The bacterium produces proteins that, when ingested, kill lepidopteran caterpillars. The gene encoding for these highly toxic proteins, when introduced into the host plant genome, confers resistance against caterpillars, when the same toxic proteins are produced within the plant. This approach is controversial, however, due to the possibility of ecological and toxicological side effects.

Pharmaceutical

Many currently available pharmaceuticals are derived from the secondary metabolites plants use to protect themselves from herbivores, including opium, aspirin, cocaine, and atropine These chemicals have evolved to affect the biochemistry of insects in very specific ways. However, many of these biochemical pathways are conserved in vertebrates, including humans, and the chemicals act on human biochemistry in ways similar to that of insects. It has therefore been suggested that the study of plant-insect interactions may help in bioprospecting

There is evidence that humans began using plant alkaloids in medical preparations as early as 3000 B.C Although the active components of most medicinal plants have been isolated only recently (beginning in the early 19th century) these substances have been used as drugs throughout the human history in potions, medicines, teas and as poisons. For example, to combat herbivory by the larvae of some Lepidoptera species, Cinchona trees produce a variety of alkaloids, the most familiar of which is quinine. Quinine is extremely bitter, making the bark of the tree quite unpalatable, it is also an anti-fever agent, known as Jesuit's bark, and is especially useful in treating malaria.

Throughout history mandrakes (*Mandragora officinarum*) have been highly sought after for their reputed aphrodisiac properties. However, the roots of the mandrake plant also contain large quantities of the alkaloid scopolamine, which, at high doses, acts as a central nervous system depressant, and makes the plant highly toxic to herbivores. Scopolamine was later found to be medicinal use in pain management before and during labor; in smaller doses it is used to prevent motion sickness One of the most well-known medicinally valuable terpenes is an anticancer drug, taxol, isolated from the bark of the Pacific yew, *Taxus brevifolia*, in the early 1960s.

Plant Medicines

Introduction

Plant medicines are the most widely used medicines in the world today. A full eighty-five percent (85%) of the world's population employs herbs as their primary medicines. And while drugstore shelves in the US are stocked mostly with synthetic remedies, in other parts of the world the situation is quite different. In Germany, pharmacies dispense herbs prescribed by physicians.

For 5.1 billion people worldwide, natural plant-based remedies are used for both acute and chronic health problems, from treating common colds to controlling blood pressure and cholesterol. Not so long ago, this was true in the US as well. As late as the early 1950's, many of the larger pharmaceutical companies still offered a broad variety of plant-based drugs in tablet, liquid and ointment forms.

Plants are the original source materials for as many as 40% of the pharmaceuticals in use in the United States today. This is to say that either the drugs currently contain plant-derived materials, or synthesized materials from agents originally derived from plants. Some medicines, such as the cancer drug Taxol (from *Taxus brevifolia*) and the anti-malarial quinine from *Cinchona pubescens* and are manufactured from plants. Other medicinal agents such as pseudoephedrine originally derived from *ephedra* species, and menthol and methylsalicylate, originally derived from mentha species and wintergreen (*gaultheria procumbens*) respectively, are now synthesized.

Herbal use 60,000 Years Ago

Neanderthals lived from about 200,000 years ago until roughly 30,000 years ago in Europe and western Asia. They coexisted with modern humans for most of the period but then mysteriously vanished. Physical evidence of use of herbal remedies goes back some 60,000 years to a burial site at Shanidar Cave, Iraq, in which a Neanderthal man was uncovered in 1960. He had been buried with eight species of plants, seven of which are still used for medicinal purposes today.

On September 19, 1991, one of the most extraordinary discoveries of our Century took place in Austria's Otzal Alps, when two hikers discovered an ice mummy preserved by freezing. The analysis of samples of organic tissues has determined that the Iceman lived between 3350 and 3100 B.C.

The Ice Man died approximately 5200 years ago. At death he was between 40 and 50 years old and suffered from a number of medical conditions. He turned into a mummy accidentally almost immediately by the freezing weather conditions that turned him into the Ice Man. The Ice Man's possessions have given scientists a better look at what life was during the Neolithic Age in Europe. Perhaps the most valuable possession, according to many scientists, was his "medicine kit," two walnut-sized lumps of a birch fungus used as a laxative and as a natural antibiotic.

Patent Laws Drive Medicinal Development

The replacement of herbs with synthetic drugs is a relatively new phenomenon, less than a century old, born largely out of economic opportunities afforded by patent laws. Drug companies can't typically patent commonly used plants, but they can develop patented, proprietary synthetic drugs, often reaping billions in sales. Since the 1940s, chemists employed by pharmaceutical companies have developed novel synthetic molecules which have replaced plant medicines, and are sold both over the counter and by prescription.

Drugs are often Dangerous

The results of this synthetic drug explosion have been unfortunate. Today, drugs prescribed in hospitals constitute the number six cause of death among American adults. This exceeds deaths due to crack, handguns, and traffic accidents combined. Add to that figure the number of adult and child deaths attributable to over the counter and prescription drugs given outside of hospitals, and the figures are even worse.

Plant Medicines, Safer and Time-tested

Plant medicines are far and away safer, gentler and better for human health than synthetic drugs. This is so because human beings have co-evolved with plants over the past few million years. We eat plants, drink their juices, ferment and distill libations from them, and consume them in a thousand forms. Ingredients in plants, from carbohydrates, fats and protein to vitamins and minerals, are part of our body composition and chemistry.

Plants and Humans Share Similarities

Some compounds perform the same functions in plants and in the body. Natural antioxidant phenols in plants, for example, protect plant cells from oxidation, and often perform the same function in the human body. Our bodies recognize the substances that occur in plants, and possess sophisticated mechanisms for metabolizing plant materials.

Synthetic Drugs are Foreign to the Body

The same cannot be said about synthetic drugs. These agents are most often alien to the chemistry of thc human body, and are separate and apart from the careful crafting of evolution. Synthetic drugs often act in the body as irritants and toxins, upsetting the balance of whole systems, producing side effects that can be lethal. By contrast, the regular and judicious use of herbs to protect and promote health and as medicines to help treat common ailments is an enlightened approach to personal well-being.

Plants can be Dangerous too

Plants can also pose a danger to human health. Drink a tea made from oleander leaves or chew a mouthful of foxglove and you'll be dead in a hurry. On the other hand, if you use any of the thousands of healthful herbs that have been utilized as traditional medicines over the past few millenia, in dosage ranges that have been determined by centuries of trial and error, you are likely to benefit without side effects.

What Are Herbs?

The term "herbs" refers to plants or parts of them, including grasses, flowers, berries, seeds, leaves, nuts, stems, stalks and roots, which are used for their therapeutic and health- enhancing properties. Generations of skilled herbal practitioners, researchers and scholars have refined and tested the vast science of herbology, producing thousands of plant-based remedies that are safe and effective. The proper and judicious use of herbs is often successful in the treatment of illness when other, more conventional medicines and methods fail. Herbs can be used to cleanse the bowels, open congested sinuses, help mend broken bones, stimulate the brain, increase libido, ease pain, aid digestion, and a thousand other purposes. Topically, herbs can repair damaged skin, soothe a wound, improve complexion, heal bruises and relieve aching muscles. Herbs demonstrate great versatility for the treatment of a broad variety of health needs.

Drugs of Plant Origin

Senna alexandrina, a shrubby perennial native to Arabia, was introduced as a laxative to Europe by Arab physicians in the ninth century. Preparations of the plant and its cathartic pods are still widely used today in popular brands of drugstore laxatives.

Mentha (mint) species are the natural sources of menthol, an aromatic alcohol which is also known as peppermint camphor. Menthol is an active ingredient in topical preparations to relieve itching and as a mild local anesthetic to soothe soreness and ease muscular tension. Menthol is commonly used in lozenges for sore throats, and is added to inhalers to treat upper respiratory disorders and open congested sinuses. Peppermint oil, which can still be found in drugstores, is a centuries-old remedy for quelling an upset stomach.

Gaultheria procumbens, or wintergreen, is a source of methylsalicylate, which is widely used in topical ointments and liniments to relieve muscular pain, and for lumbago, sciatica and rheumatic conditions.

Papaver somniferum, the opium poppy, yields a sap of narcotic opium, from which the potent pain killer morphine is made. Seeds and capsules discovered in the four thousand year old archaeological remains of Swiss lake-dwellers suggest the use of the plant for its narcotic juice. In the eighth century Persian caravans bore both opium and its methods of euphoric use to India and China. In 1546 a French naturalist named Belon drew European attention to widespread opium abuse among Turks. Opium dens proliferated in Europe throughout the 1800's, while the opium trade became an enormous industry. Simultaneously, opium and its products heroin and morphine established themselves among drug users and in the field of medicine. Both uses continue to this day. In modern medicine, morphine and its analogues remain unsurpassed pain killers.

Digitalis purpurea, the purple foxglove, is a popular garden plant cultivated as a source of digitoxin, a cardiac drug which increases the strength of heart beat while decreasing its rate. The plant was recommended for medicinal purposes in the seventeenth century, and has appeared in the French Pharmacopoeia since its first printing in 1818. Digitoxin is used in the treatment of congestive heart failure and other cardiac disorders. *Digitalis lanata*, the woolly foxglove, is cultivated commercially as a source of digoxin, a cardiotonic used for the same purposes as digitoxin.

On a trip to Burma (Myanmar) in 1930, an Indian named M. Manal discovered that elephants in captivity were often fed a particular type of root reputed to produce a calming effect. Intrigued, Manal brought samples of the plant back to India, where he conducted tests on its properties. The plant, *Rauwolfia serpentina*, named after famous 16th century German physician and explorer Leonhart Rauwolf, demonstrated both tranquilizing and anti-hypertensive properties. These effects were due to the presence of the alkaloid reserpine. In 1934 Serpina, the world's first-ever anti-hypertensive drug, was launched. Today reserpine is used both as an antihypertensive and as a sedative to relieve some types of psychiatric disorders.

Ecuadorian *Cinchona pubescens*, a fast-growing evergreen, as well as other species of cinchona, stand among the greatest life-saving medicines of all time. According to legend this plant was brought to light in the 1620's when Ecuadorean physician Juan del Vega used a Quichua native remedy known as "quina bark" on the Countess of Chinchon, wife of the Viceroy of Peru, who had contracted malaria, a potentially fatal disease caused by a protazoan in the stomach of the female Anopheles mosquito. The Countess recovered, and "quina bark" became known as "Countess bark." Word of the cure spread, and cinchona was popularized by an apothecary's assistant named Robert Talbor in the late 1660s. Over the next 150 years a huge trade in cinchona bark developed. In the early 19th century, the Dutch established cinchona plantations in Java. In 1820, quinine was isolated from cinchona, and a successful treatment for malaria was established. Today cinchona is cultivated in several tropical regions, and the approximately 10,000 tons of bark harvested annually yields 500 tons of quinine and related alkaloids quinidine, cinchonine, and cinchonidine.

Members of Columbus' second trip to the Americas in 1493 were the first to experience curare, a poison on the tips of arrows which killed them promptly. Sir Walter Raleigh, on his 1595 voyage up the Orinoco River encountered similar poisoned arrows, and launched a legend which spawned the quest to find the source of the poison. In 1799, explorer Baron von Humboldt witnessed a shaman preparing arrow poison from a vine. Von Humbldt brought some of the poison back to Europe, where it stupefied and asphyxiated animals subjected to it. Subsequent explorers attempted to find and identify the plant, but could not do so until 1938, when an American named Richard Gill found and successfully identified *Chondodendron tomentosum*, the source of curare. This led to the development of the valuable drug tubocurarine, which is used as an adjunct to general anaesthesia, and in cases of spastic paralysis and plastic muscular rigidity.

In cancer treatment, the drug Paclitaxel (Taxol) a derivative of the Pacific yew *Taxus brevifolia*, is used in chemotherapy.

The Madagascar periwinkle *Catharanthus roseus*, is the source of vinblastine and vincristine, alkaloids used respectively in the treatment of Hodgkin's disease and pediatric leukemia.

Ergot, or *Claviceps purpurea*, is a toxic fungus which grows on rye kernels, and yields several valuable alkaloids including ergotamine, which is used to treat migraine. Interestingly enough, ergot also yields lysergic acid, a derivative of which is $C_{20}H_{25}N_3O$, or LSD (lysergic acid diethylamide). First made by chemist Albert Hofmann in the laboratories of Sandoz Pharmaceuticals in Basel, Switzerland in 1938, LSD's effects were discovered accidentally by Hofmann in 1943. LSD subsequently became the cornerstone drug of the 1960s psychedelic revolution, and one of the most influential drugs in history.

Plants and their derivatives are currently the sources for thousands of drugs worldwide. But this does not mean that they are all safe or side-effect free. Isolated principles from plants such as morphine, reserpine, digitoxin, vincristine and vinblastine are toxic, due in part to their tremendous concentration.

Plant medicines remain indispensable to modern pharmacology and clincial practice. Much of the current drug discovery and development process is plant-based, and new medicines derived from plants are inevitable.

The other Side of Plant Medicines

On this web site, you will encounter a great deal of information about the non-pharmaceutical side of plant medicines. Today, you can acquire botanicals at pharmacies, natural product stores, and supermarkets. The proliferation of plant medicines is steadily on the increase. Today, plant medicines account for over $60 Billion in sales worldwide, according the World Health Organization.

On this site, you can learn about kava, maca, tamanu, Rhodiola rosea, Tongkat Ali, and a plethora of safe, effective plant medicines. In this way, you will become better informed, and will learn to more fully appreciate the critically important role that plant medicines play in health and culture.

Major Groups of Chemicals for Plant Disease Control

Plant diseases caused by parasitic microorganisms such as fungi, bacteria, mycoplasma, viruses, and nematodes may sometimes be controlled through the use of chemicals. Chemicals that kill or retard fungi are fungicides, those that control bacteria and mycoplasma are bactericides, and those controlling nematodes are nematicides. Virus diseases cannot be controlled with chemicals. Since most plant diseases are caused by fungi, the majority of the chemicals listed her are fungicides. Fortunately, most of the fungicides and bactericides have low mammalian toxicity and do not present serious health hazards.

Most chemicals used to control plant diseases are "protectants" and must be applied before infection to protect the plant from invasion by a pathogen. A few chemicals are termed "eradicants" since they can eliminate an established infection. Some newer fungicides are systemics, meaning that they are absorbed by the foliage or roots and move within the plant to the site of infection. Systemic chemicals may be protectants, eradicants, or both.

The chemicals listed are grouped according to the active chemical component or chemical base. Only a few representative chemicals are included for each group. The names used are generally the common chemical names, not the commercial or trade names. Compounds accompanied by an asterisk (*) are no longer available for use in the United States.

INORGANIC FUNGICIDES

Sulfur Fungicides

Sulfur, in many forms, i.e. elemental sulfur, wellable sulfur, flowable sulfur and line sulfur is the oldest effective fungicide known and is still very effective for some diseases. It is available as a sulfur dust for control of powdery mildew; a wettable powder for control of foliar fruit diseases; and lime sulfur which is frequently used as an eradicant. Sulfur can cause damage to some plants and cannot be used when temperatures exceed 80-90° F.

Copper Fungicides

Forms of Copper fungicides:–

Bordeaux mixture, copper sulfate, copper oxychloride, cupric oxide, basic copper sulfate, cupric carbonate and copper hydroxide.

This group includes inorganic copper compounds which are practically insoluble in water. The copper ion provides the fungicidal as well as the phytotoxic properties of these compounds. The insolubility of these compounds allows for release of only low levels of copper, adequate for fungicidal activity but not enough to affect the plant. Because of their insolubility, they are not easily washed off by rain. They are relatively safe to use because of their low toxicity to animals and humans. With the exception of Bordeaux mixture and copper sulfate, they are often called fixed coppers. Some of the fungicides are also used to control bacterial diseases and as algaecides in waterways and ponds.

ORGANIC FUNGICIDES

The era of organic fungicides began in 1934 and has since played a major role in the world-wide control of plant diseases. They are generally more effective and less toxic than the inorganic compounds.

Carbamates

Ferbam*, maneb, maneb, zineb, mancozeb, thiram and ziram.

This group of fungicides has been the most important, most versatile and most widely used of the fungicides. Most contain a metal ion attached to an organic molecule derived from dithiocarbamic acid. They are chiefly used as foliar protectants, although thiram is a seed treatment.

Dicarboximides

Captan, folpet*, captafol*, iprodione, vinclozolin.

Captan, folpet and captafol are extremely useful, wide-spectrum fungicides with low toxicity to plants and animals. They have been used primarily as foliage dusts and sprays on fruits, vegetables, and ornaments. However, because they are probably carcinogens, these older dicarboximides are gradually being withdrawn. The newer dicarboximides—iprodione and vinclozolin–are loosely related to captan, folpet and captafol but do not have as broad an action spectrum and are much more prone to the development of resistance by target fungi. However, they are quite useful against certain fungi, especially those whose cause brown rot in stone fruit and white mold in vegetables.

Substituted Aromatics

Hexachlorobenzene, pentachlorobenzene, chloroneb,* pentachlorophenol, ethazole (etridiazole)

This is a rather arbitrary classification assigned to the benzene-derived fungicides which exhibit cross-resistance with the dicarboximide fungicides. Most are used as seed and soil treatments while others are used as foliage-protectant fungicides. Pentachlorophenol is used as a wood preservative as well as an herbicide.

Organic Coppers

Copper resinate, copper oleate*, copper oxinate, copper linoleate.

These are generally used as foliar protectants. They are usually less toxic to plants than the inorganic coppers. Some of these organic copper fungicides are also used for control of bacterial diseases such as fire blight.

ANTIBIOTICS

Antibiotics are organic compounds produced by microorganisms which inhibit or kill other microorganisms. Penicillin is an antibiotic commonly used for treating human diseases caused by bacteria. Antibiotics are also used in agriculture for control of bacterial and mycoplasma diseases.

Streptomycin is used as a dust or spray to control fire blight and soft rots of vegetables. *Terramycin* is used as a therapeutic injection to control mycoplasma diseases (e.g., western X of cherry and pear decline). Both are relatively non-toxic to mammals.

SYSTEMIC FUNGICIDES

These fungicides are absorbed by the plant and carried by translocation to various parts of the plant. Many of these chemicals have eradicant properties. A few of the systemics can be applied as soil treatments and are slowly absorbed through the roots. These fungicides are the most recently developed and are the most promising type of fungicide for the future. However, because systemic fungicides often have a specific site of action in the target fungus, fungi may readily develop resistance to them if they are not managed appropriately. Most systemic fungicides are not available for home use.

Benzimidazoles

These are effective against a broad spectrum of plant diseases including powdery mildew, Botrytis and Fusarium. They have both protective and eradicative properties. Their use may be limited, however, because resistance has been noted in several species of fungi. Benomyl (Benlate) has been withdrawn for home garden, landscape, and commercial greenhouse use.

Oxatlaiins

These are very effective seed treatments for control of smuts, rusts, and other Basidiomycetes on cereal crops.

Sterol Inhibitors

Compounds in this large group inhibit sterol synthesis in sensitive fungi, especially rusts and mildews. They possess varied chemical structures but are all active at fairly low rates and with low mammalian toxicity. Some have eradicative activity against some fungi.

Strobilurins

This is a new group of fungicides with broad spectrum activity against fungi, but is not registered on many crops due to its recent introduction onto the market. Strobilurins are locally systemic (mesosystemic) with translaminar activity. Fungicides in this class affect the electron transport chain in fungi mitochondria, causing energy production necessary for fungal metabolism to cease.

FUMIGANTS

These chemicals are unrelated, but the compounds are similar in that they are highly volatile with fumigant action. Most are biocides, e.g., they kill all soil-borne microbes, nematodes, and weeds. They are also very toxic to mammals. None of these are available for home use.

Photoperiodism

Response by an animal or plant to changes in daily, seasonal, or yearly cycles of light and darkness. Among animals, sleep, migration, reproduction, and the changing of coats or plumage are regulated to some extent by day length. In the poultry industry, photoperiodism is commonly induced by artificial lighing to maximize egg laying and body weight. Plant growth, seed setting, germination, flowering, and fruiting are also affected by day length. Other environmental factors that modify an organism's responses include temperature and nutrition.

The growth, development, or other responses of organisms to the length of night or day or both. Photoperiodism has been observed in plants and animals, but not in bacteria (prokaryotic organisms), other single-celled organisms, or fungi.

A true photoperiodism response is a response to the changing day or night. Some species respond to increasing day lengths and decreasing night lengths (for example, by forming flowers or developing larger gonads); this is called a long-day response. Other species may exhibit the same response, or the same species may respond in some different way, to decreasing days and increasing nights; this is a short-day response. Sometimes a response is independent or nearly independent of day length, and is said to be day-neutral. There are many plant responses to photoperiod. These include development of reproductive structures in lower plants (mosses) and in flowering plants; rate of flower and fruit development; stem elongation in many herbaceous species as well as coniferous and deciduous trees (usually a long-day response and possibly the most widespread photoperiodism response in higher plants); autumn leaf drop and formation of winter dormant buds (short days); development of frost hardiness (short days); formation of roots on cuttings; formation of many underground storage organs such as bulbs (onions, long days), tubers (potato, short days), and storage roots (radish, short days); runner development (strawberry, short day); balance of male to female flowers or flower parts (especially in cucumbers); aging of leaves and other plant parts; and even such obscure responses as the formation of foliar plantlets (such as the minute plants formed on edges of *Bryophyllum* leaves), and the quality and quantity of essential oils (such as those produced by jasmine plants). Note that a single plant, for example, the strawberry, might be a short-day plant for one response and a long-day plant for another response.

Many angiosperms flower at about the same time every year. This occurs even though they may have started growing at different times. Their flowering is a response to the changing length of day and night as the season progresses. The phenomenon is called photoperiodism. It helps promote cross pollination.

In 1920 two employees of the U.S. Department of Agriculture, W.W. Garner and H.A. Allard, discovered a mutation in tobacco — a variety called Maryland Mammoth — that prevented the plant from flowering in the summer as normal tobacco plants do. Maryland Mammoth would not bloom until late December.

Experimenting with artificial lighting in winter and artificial darkening in summer, they found that Maryland Mammoth was affected by photoperiod. Because it would flower only when exposed to short periods of light, they called it a short-day plant. Some other short-day plants are:

- chrysanthemums (bloom in the fall)
- rice (*Oryza sativa*)
- poinsettias
- morning glory (*Pharbitis nil*)
- the cocklebur (*Xanthium*)

Some plants such as:

- spinach
- Arabidopsis;
- sugar beet; and
- radish.

Flower only after exposure to long days and hence are called long-day plants.

Still other plants, e.g. the tomato, are day neutral; that is, flowering is not regulated by photoperiod.

Photoperiodism also explains why some plant species can be grown only in a certain latitude.

- Spinach, a long-day plant, cannot flower in the tropics because the days never get long enough (14 hours).
- Ragweed, a short-day plant, fails to thrive in northern Maine because by the time the days become short enough to initiate flowering, a killing frost in apt to occur before reproduction and the formation of seeds is completed.

Photoperiodism in a Short-day Plant

Experiments with the cocklebur have shown that the term short-day is something of a misnomer; what the cocklebur needs is a sufficiently long night.

- Cocklebурs (adapted to the latitude of Michigan) will flower only if they have been kept in the dark for at least 8.5 hours — the critical period. (A and B).
- Interruption of an otherwise long night by light — red (660 nm) rays are particularly effective — prevents flowering. (C) unless
- it is followed by irradiation with far red (730 nm) light (D).
- An intense exposure to far red light at the start of the night reduces the dark requirement by 2 hours (E).

These response are mediated by phytochrome.

Phytochrome

- Phytochrome is a homodimer: two identical protein molecules each conjugated to a light-absorbing molecule (compare rhodopsin).
- Plants make 5 phytochromes: PhyA, PhyB, as well as C, D, and E.
- There is some redundancy in function of the different phytochromes but there also seem to be functions that are unique to one or another. The phytochromes also differ in their absorption spectrum; that is, which wavelengths (e.g., red vs. far-red) they absorb best.
- Phytochromes exist in two interconvertible forms
  - PR because it absorbs red (R; 660 nm) light;
  - PFR because it absorbs far red (FR; 730 nm) light.
- These are the relationships:
  - Absorption of red light by PR converts it into PFR.
  - Absorption of far red light by PFR converts it into PR.
  - In the dark, PFR spontaneously converts back to PR.

The Hourglass Model

The behavior of phytochrome provided the first model — called the hourglass model — of the mechanism of photoperiodism in short-day plants.

- Sunlight is richer in red (660 nm) than far-red (730 nm) light, so at sundown all the phytochrome is PFR.
- During the night, the PFR converts back to PR.
- The PR form is needed for the release of the flowering signal.

Therefore, the cocklebur needs 8.5 hours of darkness in which to:

- convert all the PFR present at sundown into PR
- carry out the supplementary reactions leading to the release of the flowering signal ("florigen").
- If this process is interrupted by a flash of 660-nm light, the PR is immediately reconverted to PFR and the night's work is undone (C)
- A subsequent exposure to far-red (730 nm) light converts the pigment back to PR and the steps leading to the release of "florigen" can be completed (D)
- Exposure to intense far-red light at the beginning of the night sets the clock ahead about 2 hours or so by eliminating the need for the spontaneous conversion of P_{FR} to P_R (E).

Problems with the Hourglass Model

The hourglass model fails to account for the fact that nighttime exposure to red light works even after two hours of darkness when all the PFR has already been converted to PR. Recent work—mostly in the long-day plant, Arabidopsis—supports a different model of photoperiodism. This work suggests that the photoperiodic response is governed by the interaction of:

- daylight with
- innate circadian rhythms of the plant.

The Circadian Rhythm Model

- Virtually all eukaryotes have innate circadian rhythms.
- These are rhythms of biological activities that fluctuate over a period of approximately 24 hours (L. *circa* = about; *dies* = day) even under constant environmental conditions (e.g. continuous darkness). Under constant conditions, the cycles may drift out of phase with the environment.
- However, when exposed to the environment (e.g., alternating day and night), the rhythms become entrained; that is, they now cycle in lockstep with the cycle of day and night with a period of exactly 24 hours.

In Arabidopsis, the entrainment of the rhythms requires that light is detected by the:

- phytochromes (absorb red light); and
- cryptochromes (absorb blue light).

Long-Day Plants

Arabidopsis is a long-day plant and has provided many clues about the mechanism involved in this photoperiodic response.

Any response to photoperiod requires a method of keeping time; that is, a clock. Plants, like so many other organisms, have an innate circadian rhythm that regulates the expression of many genes.

Among these in Arabidopsis is *Constans* (*CO*), a gene that encodes a zinc-finger transcription factor whose levels of mRNA rise and fall with a circadian rhythm.

Translation of constans mRNA produces the transcription factor that turns on a number of genes, including *Flowering Locus T* (*FT*), a gene needed to start the conversion of apical buds in flower buds.

Constans messenger RNA (mRNA)

- is abundant early in the morning;
- declines during the middle part of the day; and
- rises to another peak late in the afternoon.

However,

- the Constans protein is quickly degraded (in proteasomes) during the morning and middle part of the day and also during the night.
- The degradation triggered by morning light (rich in 660 nm rays) is mediated by phytochrome B (PhyB);
- By late in the afternoon, if the day has been long enough;
- transcription of the *CO* gene increases producing a rise in CO mRNA;
- translation of the CO mRNA produces more CO protein which is no longer degraded.

These effects are mediated by the absorption of:

- red (enriched in far-red) light by phytochrome A (PhyA); and
- blue light by cryptochrome.

Now with the Constans protein accumulating, it is available to turn on the gene transcription (e.g., *FT*) needed for the induction of the flowering.

In short days, with darkness falling before the rise in Constans mRNA, there is not enough Constans protein synthesized to induce flowering.

So flowering in Arabidopsis seems to require the interaction of:

- daylight perceived by phytochromes and cryptochromes;
- the intrinsic circadian rhythm of Constans expression.

Short-Day Plants

The roles of circadian rhythms and light in short-day plants are not yet as well understood. Studies with rice, a short-day plant, suggests that the mechanism described for Arabidopsis may work there as well but with Constans acting as a suppressor of *Flowering Locus T* and thus as an inhibitor of flowering under long days.

Trees

Photoperiodism not only controls flowering in some trees but also stops vegetative growth and promotes the setting of winter buds as the days grow shorter in the autumn. In aspens (*Populus* sp.) this control is mediated by Constans and Flowering Locus T.

Animal Responses

There are also many responses to photoperiod in animals, including control of several stages in the life cycle of insects (for example, diapause) and the long-day promotion in birds of molting, development of gonads, deposition of body fat, and migratory behaviour. Even feather color may be influenced by photoperiod (as in the ptarmigan). In several mammals the induction of estrus and spermatogenic activity is controlled by photoperiod (sheep, goat, snowshoe hare), as is fur color in certain species (snowshoe hare). Growth of antlers in American elk and deer can be controlled by controlling day length. Increasing day length causes antlers to grow, whereas decreasing day length causes them to fall off. By changing day lengths rapidly, a cycle of antler growth can be completed in as little as 4 months; slow changes can extend the cycle to as long as 2 years. When attempts are made to shorten or extend these limits even more, the cycle slips out of photoperiodic control and reverts to a 10-12-month cycle, apparently controlled by an internal annual "clock."

Seasonal Responses

Response to photoperiod means that a given manifestation will occur at some specific time during the year. Response to long days (shortening nights) normally occurs during the spring, and response to short days (lengthening nights) usually occurs in late summer or autumn. Since day length is accurately determined by the Earth's rotation on its tilted axis as it revolves in its orbit around the Sun, detection of day length provides an extremely accurate means of determining the season at a given latitude. Such other environmental factors as temperature and light levels also vary with the seasons but are clearly much less dependable from year to year.

Mechanisms

It has long been the goal of researchers on photoperiodism to understand the plant or animal mechanisms that account for the responses. Light must be detected, the duration of light or darkness must be measured, and this time measurement must be metabolically translated into the observed response: flowering, stem elongation, gonad development, fur color, and so forth. Basic mechanisms differ not only between plants and animals but among different species as well. The roles (synchronization, anticipation, and so on) are similar in all organisms that exhibit photoperiodism, but the mechanisms through which these roles are achieved are apparently quite varied.

Strongest inhibition of flowering in short-day plants comes when the light interruption occurs around the time of the critical night (about 7-9 h for cocklebur plants), but actual effectiveness also depends on the length of the dark period. With short-day cockleburs, the shorter the night, the less the flowering and the longer the time that light inhibits flowering.

Orange-red wavelengths used as a night interruption are by far the most effective part of the spectrum in inhibition of short-day responses and promotion of long-day responses (flowering in most studies), and effects of orange-red light can be completely reversed by subsequent exposure of plants to light of somewhat longer wavelengths, called far-red light. These observations led in the early 1950s to discovery of the phytochrome pigment system, which is apparently the molecular machinery that detects the light effective in photoperiodism of higher plants.

In photoperiodism of short-day plants, an optimum response is usually obtained when phytochrome is in the far-red receptive form during the day and the red-receptive form during the night. Although normal daylight contains a balance of red and far-red wavelengths, the red-receptive form is most sensitive, so the pigment under normal daylight conditions is driven mostly to the far-red receptive form. At dusk this form is changed metabolically, and the red-receptive form builds up. It is apparently this shift in the form of phytochrome that initiates measurement of the dark period. This is how a plant "sees": when the far-red-sensitive form of the pigment is abundant, the plant "knows" it is in the light; the red-sensitive form (or lack of far-red form) indicates to the plant's biochemistry that it is in the dark.

The measurement of time—the durations of the day or night—is the very essence of photoperiodism. The discovery of a biological clock in living organisms was made in the late 1920s. It was shown that the movement of leaves on a bean plant (from horizontal at noon to vertical at midnight) continued uninterruptedly for several days, even when plants were placed in total darkness and at a constant temperature, and that the time between given points in the cycle (such as the most vertical leaf position) was almost but not exactly 24 h. In the case of bean leaves, it was about 25.4 h. Many other cycles have now been found with similar characteristics in virtually all groups of plants and animals.

There is strong evidence that the clocks are internal and not driven by some daily change in the environment. Such rhythms are called circadian.

Circadian rhythms usually have period lengths that are remarkably temperature-insensitive, which is also true of time measurement in photoperiodism. Furthermore, the rhythms are normally highly sensitive to light, which may shift the cycle to some extent. Thus, daily rhythms in nature are normally synchronized with the daily cycle as the Sun rises and sets each day. Their circadian nature appears only when they are allowed to manifest themselves under constant conditions of light (or darkness) and temperature, so that their free-running periods can appear.

Photomorphogenesis

Plants can sense light direction, quality (wavelength), intensity and periodicity. Light induces phototropism, photomorphogenesis, chloroplast differentiation and various other responses such as flowering and germination.

Light quality is mainly sensed by the presence of different light receptors specific for different wavelengths. The red/far red photoreceptors are called phytochrome. There are at least 2 classes of blue light receptors; cryptochrome recognizes blue, green and UV-A light, while phototropin perceives blue light.

Light has profound effects on the development of plants. The light-mediated changes in plant growth and development are called photomorphogenesis. The most striking effects of light are observed when a germinating seedling emerges from the soil and is exposed to light for the first time.

Normally the seedling radicle (root) emerges first from the seed, and the shoot appears as the root becomes established. Later, with growth of the shoot (particularly when it merges into thc light) there is increased secondary root formation and branching. This coordinated progression of developmental responses are early manifestations of correlative growth phenomena where the root affects the growth of the shoot and vice versa. To a large degree, these coordinated differential growth responses are hormone mediated.

In the absence of light, plants develop an etiolated growth pattern. Etiolation of the seedling adapts it to emerging from the soil.

The developmental changes characteristic of photomorphogenesis shown by de-etiolated seedlings, are induced by light. Typically, plants are responsive to wavelengths of light in the blue, red and far-red regions of the spectrum through the action of several different photosensory systems. The photoreceptors for red and far-red wavelengths are know as phytochromes. There are at least 5 members of the phytochrome family of photoreceptors. There are several blue light photoreceptors.

Tochromes are proteins with a light absorbing pigment attached (chromophore).

The chromophore is a linear tetrapyrrole called phytochromobilin.

The phytochrome apoprotein is synthesized in the Pr form. Upon binding the chromophore, the holoprotein becomes sensitive to light. If it absorbs red light it will change conformation to the biologically active Pfr form. The Pfr form can absorb red light and switch back to the Pr form.

Most plants have multiple phytochromes encoded by different genes. The different forms of phytochrome control different responses but there is also a lot of redundancy so that in the absence of one phytochrome, another may take on the missing functions.

Arabidopsis has 5 phytochromes - PHYA, PHYB, PHYC, PHYD, PHYE.

Molecular analyses of phytochrome and phytochrome-like genes in higher plants, ferns, mosses, algae, and photosynthetic bacteria have shown that phytochromes evolved from prokaryotic photoreceptors that predated the origin of plants.

As for the red/far-red system, plants contain multiple blue light photoreceptors which have different functions.

Based on studies with action spectra, mutants and molecular analyses, it has been determined that higher plants contain at least 4, and probably 5, different blue light photoreceptors. Cryptochromes were the first blue light receptors to be isolated and characterized from any organism. The proteins use a flavin as a chromophore. The cryptochromes have evolved from microbial DNA-photolyase, an enzyme that carries out light-dependent repair of UV damaged DNA. Two cryptochromes have been identified in plants.

Cryptochromes control stem elongation, leaf expansion, circadian rhythms and flowering time. In addition to blue light, cryptochromes also perceive long wavelength UV irradiation (UV-A). Phototropin is the blue light photoreceptor that controls phototropism. It also uses flavin as chromophore. Only one phototropin has been identified so far (NPH1). Phototropin also perceives long wavelength UV irradiation (UV-A) in addition to blue light.

Recent experiments indicate that a 4th blue light receptor exists that uses a carotenoid as a chromophore. This new photoreceptor controls blue light induction of stomatal opening. However, the gene and protein have not yet been found. Other blue light responses exist that seem to function in plants that are missing the cryptochrome, phototropin and carotenoid photoreceptors suggesting that at least one more will be found. Since the cryptochromes were discovered in plants, several labs have identified homologous genes and photoreceptors in a number of other organisms, including humans, mice and flys. It appears that in mammals and flys, the cryptochromes function in entrainment of the biological clock. Indeed, in flys, a cryptochrome may be a functional part of the clock mechanism.

UV Systems

Based on various responses to UV light, it is assumed that there are UV-specific photoreceptors.

Analysis of Photomorphogenesis

Plants exhibit different growth habits in dark and light. In the dark they have elongated stems, undifferentiated chloroplasts and unexpended leaves. This is called skoto morphogenesis. Photomorphogenesis (light grown) involves the inhibition of stem elongation, the differentiation of chloroplasts and accumulation of chlorophyll, and the expansion of leaves. Thus the same stimulus causes opposite effects on cell elongation in leaves and stems. Photomorphogenesis can be induced by red, far red and blue light.

Much of our knowledge of light perception and signaling has come from genetic analyses of photomorphogenesis. Essentially two types of mutant screens have been performed:

Screens for mutants that look dark grown even in the light (ie. insensitive or unresponsive to light). These are often designated as hy mutants for hypocotyl elongated, a dark grown character. These mutants have identified the known light receptors and a couple other genes that function as positive regulators of the light responses.

Screens for mutants that look light grown even in the dark. These are designated as cop for constitutive photomorphogenic or det for de-etiolated (etiolated is a term used to describe the dark grown habit). These recessive mutants are epistatic to hy mutants indicating that they function as negative regulators of signal transduction steps downstream of the receptors. In other words, because loss of function mutations allow photomorphogenic development in the absence of the inducing signal (light), the normal function of the DET and COP genes is to repress photomorphogenesis in the dark.

PHYTOCHROME

Phytochrome is a protein containing a covalently attached chromophore. Phytochrome exists in 2 interconvertable conformations with different absorption spectra. Pfr absorbs far red and is generally the biologically active conformation. Pr absorbs red. Absorption of red light converts Pr to Pfr while absorption of far red converts Pfr to Pr. Phytochrome responses are classically defined by their red/far red reversibility. For example, lettuce seeds require light to germinate. Red light induces germination but if followed by a pulse of far red light, germination is inhibited. It also contains a domain resembling a protein kinase and has been shown to autophosphorylate, however the functional significance of this in light signal transduction is unknown.

Phytochrome can measure light quality because if light contains more red than far red light (as is the case in daytime sunlight), most phytochrome will be in the Pfr form. Phytochrome mediates a variety of photomorphogenic phenomena including leaf expansion and inhibition of stem elongation. One classic example is in the shade avoidance response of shade intolerant plants. Foliage readily absorbs red light and so in the shade of another plant there is higher amounts of far red light which will drive phytochrome to the Pr form. Pr does not inhibit stem elongation which allows shaded plants to elongate and grow to reach the sunlight.

Arabidopsis contains 5 phytochrome genes, *PHYA-E*, each with distinct but often overlapping functions. PHYA is photolabile while PHYB is light stable. Different phytochromes control different plant processes in response to different intensities of light. Responses are classified as hi-irradiance (HI), low fluence (LF) or very low fluence (VLF) based on the intensity of light required to trigger the response. Phytochrome studies are further complicated by the fact that different species show different sets of responses to given light conditions. Therefore it is difficult to draw generalizations about the functions of different phytochromes.

In the dark, phytochrome is localized to the cytoplasm. In the light, phytochrome translocates to the nucleus. Phytochrome physically interacts with at least one transcription factor, PIF3, in a light dependent manner. PIF3 is required for phytochrome mediated photomorphogenesis because antisense lines show elongated hypocotyls in the light (ie. decreased light response). PIF3 binds to G-BOX elements of light regulated genes and is required for phytochrome mediated regulation of several genes.

CRYPTOCHROME

Blue, green and UVA light are all perceived by a receptor called cryptochrome. It is a flavin protein with 2 chromophores attached, one for green, one for blue. There are 2 cryptochrome genes in arabidopsis, *CRY1* and *2*. Again, they have distinct but overlapping functions. hy4/cry1 is a nonphotomorphogenic mutant defective for the blue light receptor. CRY proteins appear constitutively nuclear, although there are indications that there may be some CRY functions in the cytoplasm too.

Cryptochrome action requires the presence of phytochrome because some phytochrome mutants are non-photomorphogenic in blue or green light. However the cryptochrome mutant is photomorphogenic in red light (with far red reversibility) indicating that phytochrome action does not require cryptochrome. Evidence suggests that phytochrome and cryptochrome physically interact. CRY protein can be phosphorylated in vitro by the protein kinase activity of PHY-A. Furthermore, PHYB and CRY2 interact in plant extracts and exhibit FRET in plant cells. CRY1 and 2 also appear to directly interact with COP1, a factor involved in the negative regulation of photomorphogenesis in the dark.

HY5

HY5 is a transcription factor that is a key regulator of photomorphogenesis in both the phy and cry pathways. *hy5* mutants show a dark grown habit in the light indicating that *HY5* is required for light response. In the light, the level of HY5 protein increases and in the dark, it declines. *HY5* mRNA increases in response to phytochrome activation but the gene does not have a G-BOX suggesting it may not be regulated by PIF3.

COP1 and the COP9 Signalsome

A large number of mutants were identified with *constitutive photomorphogenesis (cop)* or *de-etiolated (det)* phenotypes. These mutants look light grown in the dark and therefore are thought to function as negative regulators of light signal transduction pathways (ie. the signal transduction pathways are active in the absence of light). Many of these mutants encode proteins that form a large complex called the COP9 signalsome (CNS). The CNS is a nuclear complex that is similar to the 26S proteosome. This is a proteolytic complex that degrades ubiquitinated proteins.

COP1 is another protein that inhibits photomorphogenesis. In the dark, COP1 is present in the nucleus, but in the light it is only found in the cytoplasm. COP1 contains a ring-finger, which is a feature of many E3 ubiquitin ligases, which are involved in targeting proteins for 26S proteosome-mediated degredation. COP1 interacts with HY5, and in the dark HY5 protein levels show a decline that is dependent on COP1 and CNS. Thus it is hypothesized that in the dark, COP1 targets HY5 for degredation by CNS.

As mentioned, CRY1 and 2 are constitutively nuclear and also interact with COP1. It is hypothesized that CRY binding inhibits COP1 activity. Another factor that functions in phytochrome signal transduction, SPA1, also interacts with COP1. Thus, all photomorphogenetic signal transduction pathways appear to converge on COP1. Inhibition of COP1 may then allow accumulation of HY5 and the response to light.

Hormones

Several plant hormones are thought to be involved in photomorphogenesis. Pfr appears to inhibit the sensitivity of hypocotyls to GA, thus in the dark when Pfr is depleted, the hypocotyls become more sensitive to GA and elongate. However brassinolide has a much more central role in photomorphogenesis. Several of the cop and det mutants are rescuable with exogenous brassinolide (ie. they show dark grown habit in the dark). The det2 mutant of arabidopsis was cloned and has sequence homology with mammalian steroid 5a-reductase. This suggests a function of the DET2 gene product in a particular step of brassinolide biosynthesis. Similarly, the CPD gene shows a cop-like mutant phenotype, was cloned and has sequence similarity to another enzyme in testosterone biosynthesis, suggesting it functions in another step of the brassinolide pathway. Rescue experiments with pathway intermediates were consistent with the proposed functions of these genes. Thus, light appears to control photomorphogenesis by downregulating brassinolide production.

PHOTOTROPIN

Another blue light receptor is called phototropin. Arabidopsis contains 2 phototropins. These are involved in phototropism, but not photomorphogensis (hypocotyl elongation).

Phototropism is the directional growth in response to directional light. Shoots are positively phototropic (grow toward light) while roots often show negative phototropism (grow away from light). Directional light causes a redistribution of auxin in shoot tissues such that the side away from the light accumulates higher levels and grows faster, causing bending toward the light. Phototropism is controlled mainly by blue/UVA light. However the receptor is different from cryptochrome because the cry mutants are still phototropic. A mutant identified as nonphototropic hypocotyl1 (nph1), acts at the level of light perception in the phototropic response but still retains normal photomorphogenetic responses. This gene was recently renamed *Phototropin1*(*Phot1*). Arabidopsis contains two phototropin genes, *Phot1* and *Phot2*. Phot protein is another flavoprotein containing 2 flavin mononucleotide chromophores. The protein also contains a protein kinase domain and blue light induces Phot kinase activity.

Circadian Rhythm

A circadian rhythm is a roughly-24-hour cycle in the biochemical, physiological or behavioural processes of living entities, including plants, animals, fungi and cyanobacteria. The term "circadian", coined by Franz Halberg comes from the Latin *circa*, "around," and *diem* or *dies*, "day", meaning literally "approximately one day." The formal study of biological temporal rhythms such as daily, tidal, weekly, seasonal, and annual rhythms, is called chronobiology.

Circadian rhythms are endogenously generated, and can be entrained by external cues, called Zeitgebers, the primary one of which is daylight. These rhythms allow organisms to anticipate and prepare for precise and regular environmental changes.

History

The earliest known account of a circadian rhythm dates from the 4th century BC, when Eratosthenes in descriptions of the marches of Alexander the Great, described diurnal leaf movements of the tamarind tree. The first modern observation of endogenous circadian oscillation was by the French scientist Jean-Jacques d'Ortous de Mairan in the

1700s; he noted that 24-hour patterns in the movement of the leaves of the plant *Mimosa pudica* continued even when the plants were isolated from external stimuli.

In 1918 J.S. Szymanski showed that animals are capable of maintaining 24-hour activity patterns in the absence of external cues such as light and changes in temperature Joseph Takahashi discovered the genetic basis for the mammalian circadian rhythm in 1994.

Criteria

To differentiate genuinely endogenous circadian rhythms from coincidental or apparent ones, three general criteria must be met:

1. the rhythms persist in the absence of cues;
2. they persist equally precisely over a range of temperatures; and
3. the rhythms can be adjusted to match the local time.

The rhythm persists in constant conditions (for example, constant dark) with a period of about 24 hours. The rationale for this criterion is to distinguish circadian rhythms from those "apparent" rhythms which merely are responses to external periodic cues. A rhythm cannot be declared to be endogenous unless it has been tested in conditions without external periodic input.

The rhythm is temperature-compensated, i.e. it maintains the same period over a range of temperatures. The rationale for this criterion is to distinguish circadian rhythms from other biological rhythms arising due to the circular nature of a reaction pathway. At a low enough or high enough temperature, the period of a circular reaction may reach 24 hours, but it will be merely coincidental.

The rhythm can be reset by exposure to an external stimulus. The rationale for this criterion is to distinguish circadian rhythms from other imaginable endogenous 24-

hour rhythms that are immune to resetting by external cues and hence do not serve the purpose of estimating the local time. Travel across time zones illustrates the necessity of the ability to adjust the biological clock so that it can reflect the local time and anticipate what will happen next. Until rhythms are reset, a person usually experiences jet lag.

Origin

Photosensitive proteins and circadian rhythms are believed to have originated in the earliest cells, with the purpose of protecting the replicating of DNA from high ultraviolet radiation during the daytime. As a result, replication was relegated to the dark. The fungus *Neurospora*, which exists today, retains this clock-regulated mechanism. Rhythmicity appears to be as important in regulating cyclic biochemical processes within an individual, as in coordinating with the environment. This is suggested by the maintenance (heritability) of circadian rhythms in fruit flies after several hundred generations in constant laboratory conditions, as well as the experimental elimination of behavioral but not physiological circadian rhythms in quail.

The simplest known circadian clock is that of the prokaryotic cyanobacteria. Recent research has demonstrated that the circadian clock of *Synechococcus elongatus* can be reconstituted *in vitro* with just the three proteins of their central oscillator. This clock has been shown to sustain a 22-hour rhythm over several days upon the addition of ATP. Previous explanations of the prokaryotic circadian timekeeper were dependent upon a DNA transcription/translation feedback mechanism.

It is an unanswered question whether circadian clocks in eukaryotic organisms require translation/transcription-derived oscillations. For although the circadian systems of eukaryotes and prokaryotes have the same basic architecture: input-central oscillator-output, they do not share any homology. This implies probable independent origins.

In 1971, Ronald J. Konopka and Seymour Benzer first identified a genetic component of the biological clock using the fruit fly as a model system. Three mutant lines of flies displayed aberrant behavior - one had a shorter period, another had a longer one and the third had none. All three mutations mapped to the same gene, which was named *period*. The same gene was identified to be defective in the sleep disorder FASPS (Familial advanced sleep phase syndrome) in human beings thirty years later - underscoring the conserved nature of the molecular circadian clock through evolution. We now know many more genetic components of the biological clock. Their interactions result in an interlocked feedback loop of gene products resulting in periodic fluctuations that the cells of the body interpret as a specific time of the day.

A great deal of research on biological clocks was done in the latter half of the 20th century. It is now known that the molecular circadian clock can function within a single cell; i.e., it is cell-autonomous. At the same time, different cells may communicate with each other resulting in a synchronized output of electrical signaling. These may interface with endocrine glands of the brain to result in periodic release of hormones. The receptors for these hormones may be located far across the body and synchronize the peripheral clocks of various organs. Thus, the information of the time of the day as relayed by the eyes travels to the clock in the brain, and, through that, clocks in the rest of the body may be synchronized. This is how the timing of, for example, sleep/wake, body temperature, thirst, and appetite are coordinately controlled by the biological clock.

Importance in Animals

Circadian rhythms are important in determining the sleeping and feeding patterns of all animals, including human beings. There are clear patterns of core body temperature, brain wave activity, hormone production, cell regeneration and other biological activities linked to this daily cycle. In addition, photoperiodism, the physiological reaction of organisms to the length of day or night, is vital to both plants and animals, and the circadian system plays a role in the measurement and interpretation of day length.

> Timely prediction of seasonal periods of weather conditions, food availability or predator activity is crucial for survival of many species. Although not the only parameter, the changing length of the photoperiod ('daylength') is the most predictive environmental cue for the seasonal timing of physiology and behavior, most notably for timing of migration, hibernation and reproduction

Impact of Light-dark Cycle

The rhythm is linked to the light-dark cycle. Animals, including humans, kept in total darkness for extended periods eventually function with a freerunning rhythm. Each "day," their sleep cycle is pushed back or forward, depending on whether their endogenous period is shorter or longer than 24 hours. The environmental cues that each day reset the rhythms are called *Zeitgebers* (from the German, *Time Givers*) It is interesting to note that totally-blind subterranean mammals (e.g., blind mole rat *Spalax* sp.) are able to maintain their endogenous clocks in the apparent absence of external stimuli.

Freerunning organisms that normally have one consolidated sleep episode will still have it when in an environment shielded from external cues, but the rhythm is, of course, not entrained to the 24-hour light/dark cycle in nature. The sleep/wake rhythm may, in these circumstances, become out of phase with other circadian or ultradian rhythms such as temperature and digestion.

Recent research has influenced the design of spacecraft environments, as systems that mimic the light/dark cycle have been found to be highly beneficial to astronauts

Arctic Animals

Norwegian researchers at the University of Tromsø have shown that some Arctic animals (ptarmigan, reindeer) show circadian rhythms only in the parts of the year that have daily sunrises and sunsets. In one study of reindeer, animals at 70 degrees North showed circadian rhythms in the autumn, winter, and spring, but not in the summer. Reindeer at 78 degrees North showed such rhythms only autumn and spring. The researchers suspect that other Arctic animals as well may not show circadian rhythms in the constant light of summer and the constant dark of winter.

However, another study in northern Alaska found that ground squirrels and porcupines strictly maintained their circadian rhythms through 82 days and nights of sunshine. The researchers speculate that these two small mammals see that the apparent distance between the sun and the horizon is shortest once a day.

Biological Clock in Mammals

The primary circadian "clock" in mammals is located in the suprachiasmatic nucleus (or nuclei) (SCN)), a pair of distinct groups of cells located in the hypothalamus. Destruction of the SCN results in the complete absence of a regular sleep/wake rhythm. The SCN receives information about illumination through the eyes. The retina of the eyes contains not only "classical" photoreceptors but also photoresponsive retinal ganglion cells. These cells, which contain a photo pigment called melanopsin, follow a pathway called the retinohypothalamic tract, leading to the SCN. If cells from the SCN are removed and cultured, they maintain their own rhythm in the absence of external cues.

It appears that the SCN takes the information on day length from the retina, interprets it, and passes it on to the pineal gland, a tiny structure shaped like a pine cone and located on the epithalamus. In response the pineal secretes the hormone melatonin. Secretion of melatonin peaks at night and ebbs during the day.

The circadian rhythms of humans can be entrained to slightly shorter and longer periods than the Earth's 24 hours. Researchers at Harvard have recently shown that human subjects can at least be entrained to a 23.5-hour cycle and a 24.65-hour cycle (the latter being the natural solar day-night cycle on the planet Mars).

Determining the Human Circadian Rhythm

The classic phase markers for measuring the timing of a mammal's circadian rhythm are:

- melatonin secretion by the pineal gland; and
- core body temperature.

For temperature studies, people must remain awake but calm and semi-reclined in near darkness while their rectal temperatures are taken continuously. The average human adult's temperature reaches its minimum at about 05:00 (5 a.m.), about two hours before habitual wake time, though variation is great among normal chronotypes.

Melatonin is absent from the system or undetectably low during daytime. Its onset in dim light, *dim-light melatonin onset* (DLMO), at about 21:00 (9 p.m.) can be measured in the blood or the saliva. Both DLMO and the midpoint (in time) of the presence of the hormone in the blood or saliva have been used as circadian markers.

However, newer research indicates that the melatonin *offset* may be the most reliable marker. Benloucif *et al.* in Chicago in 2005 found that melatonin phase markers were more stable and more highly correlated with the timing of sleep than the core temperature minimum. They found that both sleep offset and melatonin offset were more strongly correlated with the various phase markers than sleep onset. In addition, the declining phase of the melatonin levels was more reliable and stable than the termination of melatonin synthesis.

One method used for measuring melatonin offset is to analyze a sequence of urine samples throughout the morning for the presence of the melatonin metabolite 6-sulphatoxymelatonin (aMT6s). Laberge *et al.* in Quebec in 1997 used this method in a study which confirmed the frequently found delayed circadian phase in healthy adolescents.

Outside the "Master Clock"

More-or-less independent circadian rhythms are found in many organs and cells in the body outside the suprachiasmatic nuclei (SCN), the "master clock." These clocks, called peripheral oscillators, are found in the esophagus, lung, liver, pancreas, spleen, thymus and the skin Though oscillators in the skin respond to light, a systemic influence has not been proven so far There is some evidence that also the olfactory bulb and prostate may experience oscillations when cultured, suggesting that also these structures may be weak oscillators.

Furthermore, liver cells, for example, appear to respond to feeding rather than to light. Cells from many parts of the body appear to have freerunning rhythms.

Light and the Biological Clock

Light resets the biological clock in accordance with the phase response curve (PRC). Depending on the timing, light can advance or delay the circadian rhythm. Both the PRC and the required illuminance vary from species to species and lower light levels are required to reset the clocks in nocturnal rodents than in humans.

Lighting levels that affect circadian rhythm in humans are higher than the levels usually used in artificial lighting in homes. According to some researchers the illumination intensity that excites the circadian system has to reach up to 1000 lux striking the retina. In addition to light intensity, wavelength (or colour) of light is a factor in the entrainment of the body clock. Melanopsin is most efficiently excited by blue light, 420-440 nm according to some researchers while others have reported 470-485 nm.

It is thought that the direction of the light may have an effect on entraining the circadian rhythm light coming from above, resembling an image of a bright sky, has greater effect than light entering our eyes from below.

The Myth of the 25-hour Day

Early investigators determined the human circadian period to be 25 hours or more. They went to great lengths to shield subjects from time cues and daylight, but they were not aware of the effects of indoor electric lights. The subjects were allowed to turn on light when they were awake and to turn it off when they wanted to sleep. Electric light in the evening delayed their circadian phase. These results became well known.

The Human Circadian Period

Modern research under very controlled conditions has shown the human period for adults to be just slightly longer than 24 hours on average. Czeisler *et al* at Harvard found the range for normal, healthy adults of all ages to be quite narrow: 24 hours and 11 minutes ± 16 minutes. The "clock" resets itself daily to the 24-hour cycle of the earth's rotation.

Timing of medical treatment in coordination with the body clock may significantly increase efficacy and reduce drug toxicity or adverse reactions. For example, appropriately timed treatment with angiotensin converting enzyme inhibitors (ACEi) may reduce nocturnal blood pressure and also benefit left ventricular (reverse) remodeling A number of studies have concluded that a short period of sleep during the day, a power-nap, does not have any effect on normal circadian rhythm, but can decrease stress and improve productivity.

There are many health problems associated with a disturbance in the human circadian rhythm, seasonal affective disorder (SAD), delayed sleep phase syndrome (DSPS) and other circadian rhythm disorders Circadian rhythms also play a part in the reticular activating system which is crucial for maintaining a state of consciousness. In addition, a reversal in the sleep-wake cycle may be a sign or complication of uremia azotemia or acute renal failure.

Disruption

Disruption to rhythms usually has a negative effect. Many travelers have experienced the condition known as jet lag, with its associated symptoms of fatigue, disorientation and insomnia.

A number of other disorders, for example bipolar disorder and some sleep disorders, are associated with irregular or pathological functioning of circadian rhythms. Recent research suggests that circadian rhythm disturbances found in bipolar disorder are positively influenced by lithium's effect on clock genes.

Disruption to rhythms in the longer term is believed to have significant adverse health consequences on peripheral organs outside the brain, particularly in the development or exacerbation of cardiovascular disease The suppression of melatonin production associated with the disruption of the circadian rhythm may increase the risk of developing cancer.

Circadian rhythms and clock genes expressed in brain regions outside the SCN may significantly influence the effects produced by drugs such as cocaine Moreover, genetic manipulations of clock genes profoundly affect cocaine's actions.

Index

A

Acacia trees, 158

Adamii, 82

African Violet, 77

Alaska, 205

Amaranth, 22

American Journal of Botany, 29

An Idea of a Philosophical History of Plants in 1672, 40

Anaesthesia, 172

Anatomia plantarum, 40

Anatomy of Plants in 1682 (The), 40

Anatomy of seed plants in 1960, 42

Anatomy of Woody Plants in 1917 (The), 42

Androecium, 39

Angkor Wat in Cambodia, 73

Animalia, 1

Anopheles mosquito, 172

Antibiotics, 178

Arabidopsis, 93, 185

Archaeopteris, 6

Archaeplastida, 8

Arizona, 72

Asparagus setaceus, 33

Augustin Pyrame de Candolle, 41

Austria Otzal Alps, 167

Avicennia, 70

Azadirachta indica, 163

B

Bacillus thuringiensis, 164

Bacon, Francis, 28

Bamboo and Grass in 1934, 42

Bark-Derived Phenols, 47

BCE Theophrastus, 40

Beet, 73

Betulaceae, 71

Beytrage zur Anatomie der Pflanzen, 41

Botrytis, 179

Bryophyllum, 181

Bryophytes, 1

Bryopsis plumose, 33

C

Cactus, 22

California Black Oak, 84

Calvin Cycle 138

Cancer, 121

Capsaicin, 163

Carolus linnaeus, 40

Carrot, 73

Casuarinaceae, 71

Catharanthus roseus, 173

Cell membranes, 97-124

- cellular respiration, 109
- chromatin, 100
- chromosome territories, 103-104
- euchromatin versus heterochromatin, 105
- euchromatin, 106
- export from the nucleus, 108-109
- heterochromatin, 105-106
- histone modifications, 101-102
- histone variants, 103
- import into the nucleus, 108
- integral membrane proteins, 97-98
- kissing chromosomes, 104
- nuclear envelope, 99-100
- nuclear pore complexes, 107-108
- nucleolus, 107
- nucleoplasm, 106, 109
- nucleosomes, 100-101
- peripheral membrane proteins, 98-99
- plasma membrane, 97
- transcription, 106

Cellular respiration
- chemiosmosis, 112
- citric acid cycle, 111
- electron transport chain, 111-112
- how many ATPs, 113
- mitochondria, 109-110
- mitochondrial DNA, 114

Centrosome, 119, 120-121

Chamaecytisus purpureus, 82

Charcot-Marie-Tooth disease, 119

Charles Valentine Riley, 162

Chemoreceptors, 124

Chicago, 207

Chili Pepper, 163

Chlorophyll, 125-130
- biosynthesis, 128
- chemical structure, 127
- chlorophyll and photosynthesis, 125-127
- culinary use 129
- spectrophotometry, 127-128

Chondodendron tomentosum, 172

Chrysanthemum, 163

Cinchona pubescens, 167, 171

Cinchona, 164

Circadian rhythm, 200-210
- biological clock in mammals, 205-206
- criteria, 201-202
- determining the human circadian rhythm, 206-207
- disruption, 209-210
- history, 200-201
- human circadian period, 208-209
- importance in animals, 204
  - arctic animals, 205
  - impact of light-dark cycle, 204-205
- light and the biological clock, 207-208
- myth of the 25-hour day, 208
- origin, 202-203
- outside the master clock, 207

Citrus species, 163

Claviceps purpurea, 173

Contributions to phytogenesis, 41

Cordyline, 65

Countess bark, 172

Countess of Chinchon, 172

Crematogaster, 158
Cucumber, 85
Cutaneous porphyria, 145-146
Cytochromes, 147
Cytokinin, 67
Cytoskeleton, 116
- actin filaments, 116-117
- centrioles, 122
- centrosomes and cancer, 121
- cilia and flagella, 122-123
- intermediate filaments, 117
- microtubule motors, 118-119
- microtubules, 118
- other functions of centrosomes, 120-121
- primary cilia, 123
  - chemoreceptors, 124
  - mechanoreceptors, 123
  - photoreceptors, 124

D

Dark Reaction Carbon-Fixing Reactions, 138
Derris, 163
Devonian plants, 151
Devonian, 2
Digitalis lanata, 171
Digitalis purpurea, 171
DNA, 102
Dracaena, 65
Drosophila, 103
Drugs, 14

E

Eggplant, 85
Endosperm, 96
Environments, 2
Erlandson, 82
Ernst Munch in 1930, 50
Euphorbia, 33

F

Fabaceae, 71
Father of Plant Physiology, 28
Felix Hoppe-Seyler in 1874, 144
Festuca arundinacea, 13, 158
Fossil Forest at Victoria Park in Glasgow, 6
Fossil fuels, 140
Fossils of sporangia, 151
Fragaria, 70
Fungicides, 177
Fusarium, 179

G

Gaultheria procumbens, 167, 170
Geotropism, 26
Gibberella fujikuroi, 93
Gibberellins, 23
Gill, Richard, 172
Global warming, 140
Glossopteris, 6
Gramineae, 42
Greenhouse Effect, 140
Gregor Mendel laws of genetics, 15
Gynoecium, 39

H

Heartwood and sapwood, 40
Hedera, 70
Heliconius, 157
Hemoglobin, 147
Herbivores, 163

Herbivory, 149-165
Homologus, 32

I

IAA, 77
IBA, 77
Ice Man, 167
Inorganic fungicides
 copper fungicides, 176
 sulfur fungicides, 176
Introduction, 1-16
 algae and fungi, 3-4
 algae, 7-8
 current definitions of plant, 7
 diversity, 9
 embryophytes, 1-3
 fossils, 5-7
 fungi, 8-9
 growth, 4-5
 importance, 4
 life processes, 9
  aesthetic uses, 15
  distribution, 12
  ecological relationships, 12-13
  ecology, 11-12
  factors affecting growth, 10-11
  food, 14
  growth, 9-10
  importance, 13-14
  internal distribution, 11
  negative effects, 16
  non-food products, 14-15
  scientific and cultural uses, 15-16

J

Journal of Experimental Botany, 29
Journal of Plant Nutrition and Proceedings of the National Academy of Sciences, 29
Juan del Vega, 172

K

Kava, 174
Kingdoms Vegetabilia, 1

L

Laburnum anagyroides, 82
LEA (Late Embryogenesis Abundant), 11
Lehrbuch der Botanik, 28
Lepidodendron, 6
Lepidoptera species, 164
Light Independent Process, 135, 136
Lonchocarpus spp., 73
Lymphoblastic leukemia, 94

M

Maca, 174
Macaranga, 158
Major groups of chemicals for plant diseases control, 175-179
 inorganic fungicides, 176
Malaria, 164
Mammoth, Maryland, 181
Mandragora officinarum, 165
Marijuana, 16
Mendel, Gregor, 15
Menthe (mint), 170
Mesopotamia, 79
Mesozoic phenomenon, 151
Michigan, 183

Mimosa pudica, 156, 201
Mitochondria, 109-110
Mixed porphyria, 148
Morphological study in 1925, 42
Motichondria, 112
Myoglobin, 147
Mythology, 16

N

NAA, 77
National Cherry Blossom Festival, 15
Nehemiah Grew, 40
Neolithic Age in Europe, 167
Neotyphodium coenophialum, 13
Neurospora, 202

O

Opium dens, 171
Organic fungicides, 177
  carbamates, 177
  dicarboximides, 177
  organic coppers, 178
  substituted aromatics, 177-178
Oriented Strand Board (OSB), 47
Origin of species, 42
Orinoco River, 172
Oryza sativa, 182

P

Pacific yew, 165
Paclitaxel (Taxol), 173
Pandanus, 65
Papaver somniferum, 170
Parsnip, 73
Passiflora, 157
Pentachlorophenol, 178
Peppermint oil, 170
Pharbitis nil, 182
Phloem, 11
Photomorphogenesis, 191-199
  analysis of photomorphogenesis, 194-195
  COP1 and the COP9 signalsome, 197-198
  cryptochrome, 196-197
  hormones, 198
  HY5, 197
  phototropin, 199
  phytochrome, 195-196
  UV systems, 194
Photoperiodism, 180-190
  animal responses, 187-188
  circadian rhythm model, 185
  constans messenger RNA, 186-187
  hourglass model, 184
  long-day plants, 185-186
  mechanisms, 188-190
  photoperiodism in a short-day plant, 182-183
  phytochrome, 183
  problems with the hourglass model, 184-185
  seasonal responses, 188
  short-day plants, 187
  trees, 187
Photosynthesis, 131-140
  C-4 pathway, 138-139
  carbon cycle, 139-140
  chlorophyll and accessory pigments, 133-135
  leaves and leaf structure, 131-133

nature of light, 133
stages of photosynthesis, 135
stages of dark reaction, 138
stages of light reactions, 136
structure of the chloroplast and photosynthetic membranes, 135
Phototropism, 26
Phylloxera, 162
Physiologia Plantarum, 29
Physiologische Pflanzenanatomie (Physiological Plant Anatomy), 41
Phytogenesis, 41
Phytotomie, 41
Pigments, 129
Pinax theatric botanici in 1596, 40
Pinus sylvestris, 46
Plant anatomy, 38, 42
history, 40-42
structural divisions, 39-40
Plant cutting, 74
advantages for grafting, 79-82
grafting, 78-79
herbaceous grafting, 85
homemade rooting supplements, 77
natural grafting, 84
providing the right humidity, 76
providing the righty soil, 76
renewing fusion, 84
rooting substance, 77
scientific uses, 84-85
stem cuttings, 78
technique, 74-75
techniques, 82
approach, 82
awl, 83
budding, 82-83
cleft, 83
stub, 83
veneer, 83-84
types of cuttings, 75-76
using rooting hormone or supplement, 77-78
Plant defense against herbivory, 149-165
carbon, 160
costs and benefits, 158-159
growth rate hypothesis, 160-161
growth-differentiation balance hypothesis, 161-162
importance to humans, 162
importance to humans: agriculture, 162-164
leaf shedding and colour, 158
optimal defense hypothesis, 159-160
pharmaceutical, 164-165
plant evolution, 150
co-evolution, 151-152
records of herbivory, 150-151
types, 152
chemical defenses, 152-153
indirect defenses, 157-158
mechanical defenses, 155-156
mimicry and camouflage, 157
thigmonasty, 156-157
types of chemical

defenses, 153-155
Plant Growth Regulators, 87
Plant hormone, 86-96
abscisic acid, 89-91
auxins, 91
characteristics, 86-88
classes of plant hormones, 88-89
cytokinins, 91-92
ethylene, 92-93
gibberellins, 93
hormones and plant propagation, 95
other known hormones, 93-94
potential medical applications, 94-95
seed dormancy, 95-96
Plant medicines, 166-174
drugs are often dangerous, 168
drugs of plant origin, 170-173
herbal use 60,000 years ago, 167
introduction, 166-167
other side of plant medicines, 173-174
patent laws drive medicinal development, 168
plant medicines, safer and time-tested, 168
plants and humans share similarities, 168-169
plants can be dangerous too, 169
synthetic drugs are foreign to the body, 169
what are herbs, 169-170
Plant morphology, 30-42
comparative science, 32
convergence, 33
homology, 32-33
plant anatomy, 38-39
scope, 30-32
vegetative and reproductive characters, 33-34
alternation of generation, 34
environmental effects, 38
juvenility, 38
morphological variation, 37
plant development, 34-36
plant growth, 36-37
positional effects, 37-38
use in identification, 34
Plant physiology, 17-29
biochemistry of plants, 19-20
constituent elements, 20-21
economic applications, 29
food production, 29
environmental physiology, 25-26
plant disease, 27
tropisms and nastic movements, 26-27
history, 28
current research, 29
early research, 28
pigments, 21-23
scope, 17-19
signals and regulators, 23
photomorphogenesis, 24
photoperiodism, 24-25
plant hormones, 23
Plant Resistance to Insects, 162
Plantae, 3

Poinsettia, 25

Populus sp., 187

Porphyria variegate, 148

Porphyria, 144

- diagnosis, 146
  - additional tests, 147
  - pathogenesis, 147-148
  - porphyrin studies, 146-147
- signs and symptoms, 145
  - acute porphyria, 145
  - *Cutaneous porphyria*, 145-146

Porphyrin, 141-148

- applications, 143-144
- biosynthesis, 143
- complexes of porphyrins and related molecules, 141-142
- laboratory synthesis, 142-143
- supramolecular chemistry, 144

PROTO oxidase, 148

Pyrethrum, 163

Q

Quercus robur, 47

Quercus suber, 46

Qunia bark, 172

R

Rauwolfia serpentine, 171

Religion, 16

Rhodiola rosea, 174

Rhynie in Aberdeenshire, 5

Root, 67-85

- economic importance, 73-74
- evolutionary history, 73
- root architecture, 72
- root growth, 68-69
- rooting depths, 72
- specialized roots, 70-71
- types of root, 69

Rutabaga, 73

S

Salix, 70

Sandoz Pharmaceuticals in Basel, 173

Sap of narcotic opium, 170

Senna alexandrina, 170

Shanidar Cave, 167

Silurian, 151

Sonneratia, 70

Species of juvenile plants, 38

Species Plantarum in 1753, 40

Strasburger, Eduard, 41

Streptomycin, 178

Studies in Fossil Botany, 41

Study of Cereal, 42

Sylva sylvarum, 28

Synechococcus elongates, 202

Systemic fungicides, 178

- benzimidazoles, 179
- fumigants, 179
- oxatlaiins, 179
- sterol inhibitors, 179
- strobilurins, 179

T

Tamanu, 174

Taxol (Taxus brevifolia), 167

Taxus brevifolia, 165, 173

Terramycin, 178

Thylakoid, 135

Tilia cordata, 46

Tomato, 85
Tongkat Ali, 174
Tradescantia zebrina, 22
Traite d' anatomie et de physiologie vegetale (Treatise on Plant Anatomy and Physiology), 41
Trifolium, 70
Turnip, 73

U

United States, 166
United States, 176
University of Tromso, 205
US Department of Agriculture, 181
US Forest Service, 63
USSR, 162

V

Variegate porphyria, 148
Viceroy of Peru, 172
Viridiplantae, 8
Virus, 85
Viscum album 71
Vitis labrusca, 162

W

Water plants, 42
Watermelon, 85
Wood anatomy, 43-66
 bark, 43
 bark chip extraction, 47
 bark removal, 47
 bark repair, 48
 botanic description, 43-45
 function, 50-51
 origin, 52
 periderm, 45-46
 phloem, 48
 rhytidome, 46
 structure, 49
  companion cells, 49-50
  girdling, 52
  sieve tubes, 49
 uses, 46-47
Wood, 52
 colour, 59-60
 different woods, 58-59
 earlywood and latewood in
  diffuse-porous woods, 64-65
  ring-porous woods, 62-64
  softwood, 61-62
 formation, 53
 growth rings, 53
 heartwood and sapwood, 55-58
 knots, 54-55
 monocot wood, 65
 structure, 60-61
 water content, 65-66
World Health Organization, 174
World War I, 42

X

Xanthium, 182
Xylem, 11
Y
Yang Cycle, 92
Young Acacias, 156

Z

Zeitgebers, 204